FAMOUS FAMILY TREES

Lincoln
Children's Books

Introduction

Family history is also world history. It tells of connections and beginnings.

Clans, tribes, and cultures can follow their histories all the way back to a common, often mythical, ancestor. Indian Sanskrit texts trace family lineages through Lord Krishna to First Man and First Woman, and Greco-Roman families gained power and prestige from having heroic ancestry.

This book tells the family histories of 25 people who lived from 100 BC to AD 2013. Some have complicated trees stretching back hundreds of years in the written record. Others, like Cleopatra, Julius Caesar, and Gandhi, have ancestors who are known only from myths, or from stories passed down orally over the years.

As you follow these trees, you'll discover that many of these family histories connect with others: Shakespeare performed for Elizabeth I; Ada Lovelace and Mary Shelley both have connections with the poet Lord Byron; and Gandhi's principles influenced Martin Luther King Jr. and Nelson Mandela.

Turn the pages to meet the families of these 25 famous faces, and see what new parts of history you can piece together, branch by branch.

IVSTI TIA   PRVD ENTIA

EOR TITV DO   TEMPE RĀTIA

The House of Hapsburg

One of the first documented family trees was one that illustrates the Austrian Hapsburg dynasty from the 13th to the 19th centuries. It features 22 sheets joined together, starting with King Pharamundo and ending with Emperor Charles V—who is seated in a tree at the trunk, his foot resting on a lion.

It was created in 1534 as a woodcut and colored using stencils. It took around a decade to complete the tree, but little is known about the artist, Peril, except that he worked in Antwerp. Around 1543, Margaret of Austria commissioned him to produce a similar frieze—this time showing the procession through Bologna that followed the coronation of Charles V as emperor.

How to use this book

The family tree is one of the most useful ways to show genealogical information—or how people relate to one another. The oldest generations sit at the top of the tree, while the youngest are at the bottom. However, a tree can also be drawn sideways as well, from left to right, with the oldest generations on the left. The diagram opposite provides more detail about how to read the family trees on the following pages.

Useful key terms

ANCESTOR: a person from whom someone descends
ANCESTRY: the entire line of people from whom someone descends, as far back as they are traceable
DESCENDANT: someone who is related to (or "descended" from) a person, or group of people, who lived in the past
MATERNAL: related through the mother (a person's "maternal ancestry" would refer to the ancestors on their mother's side)
PATERNAL: related through the father (a person's "paternal ancestry" would refer to the ancestors on their father's side)

Some of the famous faces featured in this book have families that are so big, they wouldn't fit on a single page. We have included captions for as many members of each family as possible, and added a dotted line where a generation has been jumped. See the further reading section at the back of this book for ideas of where to find out more about some of the famous people included in these pages.

A dotted line shows where we have jumped a generation.

An unbroken (usually vertical) line that drops down from the bottom of a name represents a direct descendant from a parent.

The letter "m" joins two people who are married.

Sometimes, because we are trying to fit so much history onto one page, you will need to follow the lines a little more carefully. Here, you can see that Mary was clearly married to Thomas, but we've had to fit her name underneath Elizabeth's.

The letter "c" means *circa*, which is a Latin word for "approximately." It's used when an exact date is not known. Where a birth or death date (or both) is completely unknown, you will simply see "unknown."

Horizontal lines like these show siblings from one set of parents.

John Anderson Porter I
1693-1776

Thomas A. Hoskinson, Sr.
1679-1743

Thomas Beall
1647-1730

Thomas A. Hoskinson, Jr.
1719-1802

Moses Franklin Porter
1826-1900

m

Elizabeth Ann Porter (Hoskins)
1828-1855

John Henry Porter
1849-1910

Mary Ann Beall
1722-1800

m

m

Marie Antoinette Porter
c. 1863

Ruth Mary Tall Chief (Porter)
1899-1981

Joseph Alexander Tall Chief
1890-1959

m

Marjorie Louise Tall Chief
c. 1927

Elizabeth Marie "Betty" Tallchief
1925-2013

a snippet from Maria Tallchief's family tree.

Julius Caesar

Born in 100 BC, Julius Caesar was a military ruler who led Rome from being a republic, ruled by a senate, to an empire. He descended from the strong, political Julia family and held important positions, before being exiled to the provinces. There, he wrote popular accounts of his military campaigns, which kept his fame alive in Rome. He also expanded the province of Gaul across the Channel to Britain.

Soon after, Caesar illegally returned to Rome with his army, starting a civil war that eventually made him "dictator for life." Because of his power, Caesar was considered dangerously ambitious and was assassinated in 44 BC by a group of senators, including his protégé, Brutus.

Water Crossings

Caesar's most famous military exploits involve water. He built the first-ever bridge over the Rhine, an engineering feat that intimidated and halted the German armies. He also crossed the English Channel into Britain. And his crossing of the Rubicon river in 49 BC was considered a declaration of war on Rome, which eventually led to his crowning as dictator.

The Julia Family

The ancient gens Julia family's story is one of political conflict. They were noble rulers and connected to practically everyone. Then came civil wars between Caesar's uncle-in-law, Senator Gaius Marius, and General Sulla. Sulla outlawed Caesar for not divorcing from a pro-Marius family, but his mother helped to get him pardoned. Caesar's second wife was Sulla's granddaughter. Then Caesar's daughter married his ally, Pompey, who later became his enemy...And it went on like that, for years.

Aeneas is the legendary survivor of Troy and founder of Rome. Caesar's family, the gens Julia, claims him as a divine ancestor, which gives them more power.

Aeneas (unknown)

What's in a Name?

The family name "Caesar" could mean "elephant," "to cut," or "hairy." It became a title of royalty that traveled to Russia (translated to Czar) and to Germany (translated to Kaiser).

Lucius Aurelius Cotta 169-119 BC

Rutilia 140 BC-unknown

Gaius Julius Caesar I c. 205 BC-166 BCE

Gaius Julius Caesar II c. 163 BCE

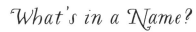

Marcia Regia 165-100 BC

Caesar's maternal grandfather was a Roman senator who was almost imprisoned for opposing the passage of a voting law.

Gaius Julius Caesar III 140-85 BC

His father died when Caesar was a teenager, forcing him to become head of the family at age 16.

Julia 130-69 BC

Caesar's paternal aunt kept her patrician (aristocratic) status, despite her husband's defeat.

From a plebian (lower class) family, he gained political power by marrying Caesar's aunt.

Gaius Marius 157-86 BC

Caesar's first and perhaps favorite wife, they were married in their teens.

Cornelia Cinnae 97-69 BC

Aurelia Cotta 120-54 BC

She was in charge of raising Caesar, since her husband was often away.

Julia Major 102-68 BC

Julia Minor 101-51 BC

Julia Minor ("the younger") is best known as the grandmother of Augustus.

Julius Caesar 100-44 BC

There are many in his family with this name, but he is referred to as "the dictator."

Pompeia 104-58 BC

Julia 76-54 BC

Caesar's only recognized legitimate child married his ally, Pompey. After her death, Pompey became Caesar's rival for power.

Caesar Augustus 63 BC-AD 14

Caesar's grand-nephew and adoptive son, he became the first official Roman emperor.

Cleopatra VII

At age 18, Princess Cleopatra VII inherited a broke and starving Egypt. Known as her father's favorite, Cleopatra was raised to rule. She grew up speaking, reading, and writing Greek, but unlike her relatives, she learned many other languages, too, including Egyptian and Latin. Soon after taking the throne, she was at war with her co-regent (co-ruler)—her brother Ptolemy XIII—and was later exiled. Meanwhile, Julius Caesar was chasing a defeated Pompey from Rome to Egypt. Ptolemy killed Pompey, hoping to win Caesar's favor. Instead, Caesar declared martial law. This was Cleopatra's chance...

She was smuggled into Caesar's room and they joined forces. After defeating their enemies, they stayed together until Caesar's assassination. It is believed that Cleopatra later died from the sting of a poisonous cobra.

Milk Baths

Cleopatra was known for her incredible beauty. One common and often-told story about Queen Cleopatra was that she took baths in donkey milk to preserve her beauty. Myth has it that nearly 700 donkeys were used to provide enough milk for her daily bath!

Floods and Famine

People have long feared floods, but Egypt depended upon the annual floods. The Nile brought rich silt to replenish the fields. Without the floods, there was famine. There were not enough floods during Cleopatra's difficult first three years, which added to her already-long list of problems.

The Ptolemaic Dynasty, 305-30 BC

Although she claimed to be the reincarnation of the Egyptian goddess Isis, Cleopatra VII was actually Macedonian. She descended from one of Alexander the Great's generals, Ptolemy I. After Alexander's death, his generals divided up the empire. Ptolemy was given Egypt and founded the last Egyptian dynasty. The Ptolemies used Egyptian titles and customs. All male rulers were renamed Ptolemy, while women were named Cleopatra, Berenice, or Arsinoe.

Heracles

Heracles is the mythical founder of the Macedonian ruling family, the Argeads.

Arsinoe of Macedon
4th century BC

Phillip II's mistress and Ptolemy's mother. Ptolemy I's father could have been Phillip II.

Ptolemy I Soter
367-283 BC

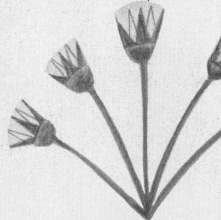

He was a trusted friend of Alexander the Great, and one of his generals and bodyguards.

Cleopatra III
161-101 BC

The longest-standing queen of Egypt, ruling for nearly 40 years.

Ptolemy X
140-88 BC

Cleopatra V
95-57 BC

Cleopatra may have descended from Ptolemy IX, or from his brother, Ptolemy X.

Berenice IV
77-55 BC

Ptolemy IX
142-81 BC

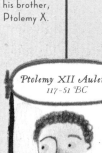

He was pharaoh three times from 116-81 BC, twice as co-regent with his mother.

Ptolemy XII Auletes
117-51 BC

When Ptolemy X's son, Ptolemy XI, was removed from the throne, Rome's financial aid helped Ptolemy XII win the position as ruler.

Arsinoe IV
63-41 BC

She became Caesar's captive and lived in the Temple of Artemis.

Ptolemy XIII Theos Philopater 62-47 BC

By killing the fugitive Pompey, Cleopatra's brother hoped to gain Julius Caesar's help in the civil war, but it did not go to plan.

Cleopatra Selene II
40-6 BC

Alexander Helios
40-29 BC

Ptolemy XVI Philadelphus
36-29 BC

In 41 BC, he became the Roman ruler of Egypt and allied himself with Cleopatra.

Mark Antony
83-30 BC

Cleopatra VII
69-30 BC

Cleopatra VII was 14 years old when she was named co-regent with her father. She was 18 when she inherited the throne along with her brother—until he exiled her.

Cleopatra and Caesar's son became Cleopatra's co-regent in 44 BC.

Ptolemy XV Philopator Philometor Caesar, Caesarion 47-30 BC

Julius Caesar,
100-44 BC

Caesar and Cleopatra became partners in the civil wars. In 46 BC, after their victories, they returned to Rome.

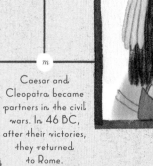

Genghis Khan

Genghis Khan (born Temujin) created one of the largest empires in history, the Mongol Empire, uniting the nomadic clans of the Central Asian steppes. Genghis banned the usual tribal sources of wars: aristocracy, kidnapping, slavery, and horse theft. Starting with China, his armies created the empire, annexing Eastern Europe, Siberia, Iran, Indochina, India, and the Levant. Genghis was brutal, but he was an excellent ruler who devised a code of ethics. To this day, people are proud to claim him as their ancestor.

True Warrior

Genghis Khan would usually give other kingdoms an opportunity to peacefully submit to Mongol rule, but he would use the sword on anyone that resisted.

Younger Years

From a young age, Genghis had to deal with brutal life on the Mongolian steppe. Rival Tatars poisoned his father when Genghis was only nine, and his own tribe expelled his family. His mother was left to raise her children alone. Genghis had to hunt and forage in order to survive, and as an adolescent, it is believed he killed his half brother in a dispute over food.

The Borjigin Family

Settled around the holy mountain of Burkhan Khaldan, the nomadic Mongols were divided into many tribes. Borjigin is Genghis Khan's family name. Starting with his merging of the tribes, the family ruled the Mongol Empire from 1206 to 1368 and continued to provide rulers into the 20th century. The ruler's title, "khan," spread throughout Asia and Turkey and continues to this day, with variant spellings.

Dobun Mergen

Dobun and Alan had two sons during their marriage.

Alan Gua c.862

Alan had three more sons after her husband's death. To promote unity between them, she told her eldest sons a story of the five arrows, which together form an unbreakable group.

Borte Khatun 1161-1230

Genghis's first wife, she had four sons and five daughters.

Bodonchar Munkhag c. 900

Alan and Dobun's youngest son. His name means "little simpleton," but he became a warlord and founded the Borjigin clan.

Genghis Khan 1162-1227

Genghis refused to have an image made during his lifetime.

Khaidu c. 1040-1100

Bodonchar's great-great-grandson and the first khan of the tribe, he was the only survivor of a Jalair raid.

Kublai Khan 1215-1294

The grandson of Genghis, he expanded the empire, choosing to live in China, where he became the first emperor. Italian trader Marco Polo visited his court.

Yesugei 1134-1171

He was Genghis's father and ruled the Hamag Mongol confederation.

Hoelun d. 1208

After her husband Yesugei's death, Hoelun made a living from the land, later becoming Genghis's trusted advisor and a caretaker of war orphans.

Ligdan Khutugtu Khan 1588-1634

He was the last Mongolian khan, ruling in Yuan Province. Allied with the Ming, he proved a brutal ruler, and after his death, the Qing took over.

Lorenzo 'De' Medici

Lorenzo de' Medici was not called "the Magnificent" because of his looks—he was shortsighted, his nose was squashed, his skin swarthy, and he had a square body and short legs. But he was a brilliant diplomat and statesman. He also had the Medici wealth to finance and support the Italian Renaissance. Florence was a republic, so Lorenzo ruled through others, buying votes and marrying his family to the right women. Florence prospered under his leadership, becoming a center of culture and art. But Lorenzo had his enemies—he nearly died in a public fight and the Pope tried to exile him. In the end, his diplomacy won out, and he maintained peace through his later life.

Banking

The Medici Bank was first founded in 1397, with branches in Rome, Geneva, Venice, and Naples. The Medici Bank became the head of finances for the Catholic Church and pioneered the "double-entry bookkeeping system" of tracking debits and credits in accounting.

Art Lover

Imagine a world without Da Vinci, Botticelli, and Michelangelo! These artists were first commissioned by Lorenzo and the Medicis, along with Donatello, Fra Angelico, Brunelleschi, and Raphael. The Medici art collections can be enjoyed today at the Uffizi Gallery. You can also view the exquisite architecture of the family home, Pitti Palace.

The Medici Family

The Medicis were a hugely wealthy Florentine banking family that practically ruled Italy for four centuries, covering financial, political, religious, intellectual, and artistic realms. They started as wool merchants. After establishing the Medici Bank, they came to govern the Republic of Florence and the Duchy of Tuscany. They fostered the Italian Renaissance, supported Galileo, and connected with other prominent families, both through marriage and business. The family tree reached over to the English kings Charles II and James II.

A Changing Coat of Arms

The Medicis belonged to the guild of money changers. They likely copied the guild's coat of arms, but with red balls replacing the Byzantine coins. The Medici motto was *Festina lente* or "Make haste slowly."

Giovanni di Bicci de' Medici c. 1360-1429
Founded the Medici dynasty with the creation of the Medici Bank.

Giovanni de' Medici, il Popolano 1467-1498
A member of the secondary branch of the Medicis, he was best known for burning "immoral" art.

Caterina Sforza 1463-1509
Countess of Forli and Lady of Imola, she was a born leader. Giovanni was her third husband.

Cosimo the Elder 1389-1464
His immense wealth controlled votes, and he ruled in the background, never taking office.

Giovanni dalle Bande Nere, the Last Condottiero 1498-1526
Employed by two Medici popes to fight in the Italian Wars, he died young from complications after his leg was amputated.

Lorenzo de' Medici, The Magnificent 1449-1492
Tutored in Humanism and Greek, he also wrote poetry in his native Tuscan language.

Cosimo I, 1st Grand Duke of Tuscany 1519-1574
By aiding Charles V in wars with France, he restored Medici control in Florence. He later became Grand Duke of Tuscany.

Eleanor of Toledo 1522-1562

King Charles II and James II of England

Alessandro, the Moor, First Duke of Florence 1510-1537
His short reign was characterized by Republican uprisings and medieval politics.

Pope Leo XI 1535-1605

Giovanni di Lorenzo de' Medici, Pope Leo X 1475-1521
Lorenzo's eldest son, Piero, became Lord of Florence, so the second one, Giovanni, became Pope! He granted money to pay for rebuilding St. Peter's Basilica.

Catherine de' Medici, Queen Consort of France 1519-1589
Married to Henry II, she served as regent for her three sons.

Giulio di Giulianode' Medici, Pope Clement VII 1478-1534
He formed the League of Cognac, which led to the Four Years' War—one of many Italian Wars.

Phillip II of Spain

Queen Elizabeth I

Elizabeth I was Queen of England more than four hundred years ago. She ruled for 45 years, in what was seen as a golden age in English history. All of England's kings and queens are related, but Elizabeth was the last member of the Tudor line. Under Elizabeth, England became a major seafaring nation, with men such as Sir Francis Drake and Sir Walter Raleigh exploring new lands and bringing back treasure. Music and literature became important in people's lives, with playwrights including William Shakespeare and Christopher Marlowe, and composers such as Thomas Tallis and William Byrd.

No Hand in Marriage

Elizabeth refused all attempts to persuade her to get married. Marriage may have meant she had children to inherit her crown. But it may also have made it harder for her to make her own decisions in an age where men were unrightly seen as superior to women...even queens.

Dressed to Impress

Elizabeth had elaborate taste in clothes—it took her serving women four hours a day to dress and undress her! She wore wigs that matched her original hair color and applied heavy makeup to mask the hair loss and scarring she suffered due to a case of smallpox.

The House of Tudor

The House of Tudor had five monarchs, or rulers, who reigned for 118 years. Their reign saw the end of the Wars of the Roses, and the change from a Catholic country to a Protestant one.

Claim to the Throne

The Tudors were of Welsh ancestry and played a lead role in the struggle to end English rule in Wales. When Henry VII defeated Richard III at the Battle of Bosworth in 1485, he declared himself king by "right of conquest."

The Tudor Rose

The Tudor rose emblem was created when Henry VII brought an end to the Wars of the Roses. He joined the white rose emblem of York with the red rose emblem of Lancaster, creating the Union rose (or Tudor rose), still used as the floral emblem of England today.

Henry VII
1457–1509
Other claimants had stronger links to the throne but Henry was victor on the battlefield.

m

Elizabeth of York
1466–1503
The first Tudor queen of England was determined to see her children rule.

Arthur Tudor
1486–1502
Arthur's birth was seen as the union of two houses— Tudor and York.

m

Catherine of Aragon
1485–1536
Married to Arthur until he died, she then became the first of Henry VIII's six wives.

m

Henry VIII
1491–1547
Best known for his six wives, Henry is England's most famous king, and the key to kick-starting the Church of England.

m

Anne Boleyn
1507–1536
Henry's second wife and the first English queen to be publicly executed.

m

Jane Seymour
1509–1537
The third of Henry's wives and the mother to his only son.

m

Anne of Cleves
1515–1557
The fourth of Henry's six wives, born in the German town of Cleves.

m

Catherine Howard
1524–1542
Cousin to Anne Boleyn, she married the king when she was just 19 years old.

m

Catherine Parr
1512–1548
The sixth wife of Henry VIII and the only one to survive him.

Mary I
1516–1558
Henry and Catherine's daughter, best-known for attempting to reverse the Protestant Reformation that began in 1517.

Elizabeth I
1533–1603
The last monarch of the House of Tudor, Elizabeth was the first to recognize that a queen should rule by popularity.

Edward VI
1537–1553
Henry's only son, who became king of England at age nine.

Margaret Tudor

James IV of Scotland

Mary Tudor

Louis XII of France

Charles, Duke of Suffolk

Frances Brandon

Henry Grey, Duke of Suffolk

James V of Scotland

Mary of Guise

Mary Queen of Scots
1542–1587
Elizabeth's cousin, whose threat to the throne put her in prison.

Lady Jane Grey
1537–1554
Remembered in history as the queen who ruled for just nine days!

William Shakespeare

Despite being the most quoted author in English literature, facts about William Shakespeare's life are sparse. He was born in Stratford-upon-Avon in 1564 and likely left for London shortly after his marriage. Shakespeare probably only came home for the forty days of Lent, when the theaters closed. By the 1590s, he was a partner of London's chief acting company, the Lord Chamberlain's Men—later the King's Men. They performed for Elizabeth I and King James I. In 1599, they built the famous Globe theater for their performances. The most revealing information about Shakespeare, can be found in his 39 plays and 154 sonnets, each one a study of humankind that transcends the time in which they were written.

Controversy over Authorship

The intellectual sophistication, beauty, and depth of Shakespeare's work has led some scholars to believe an educated member of the aristocracy must be the author. Christopher Marlow, Francis Bacon, and Edward De Vere are among the candidates. However, Shakespeare's name appears on the folios and dedications.

What's in a Name?

Documents of the time play fast and loose with spelling, and Shakespeare's name is no exception, being written as *Shakesspere, Shakysper, Shaxpeer, Schakespeire, Shackper, Shexpere, Shaxkspere,* and *Shakspeyre.* His own signature has variations, but his dedication to the Earl of Southampton is signed "Your lordship's in all duty, William Shakespeare."

The Shakespeare Family

William Shakespeare's ancestors had lived in agricultural Warwickshire for several hundred years. The Shakespeares were yeoman farmers, while the Webbs were knights. The wealthy Ardens descended from Anglo-Saxon rulers in Mercia. They kept their land after the Norman conquest, but during Elizabeth I's reign, the Catholic head of the family was executed for treason. A tangle of relationships had developed among the three families, partly due to Henry VIII—when he established the Church of England, first cousins could marry. Shakespeare's parents, John and Mary, were first cousins.

Adam of Oldiche
c. 1340-unknown

Thorkell of Arden Earl of Mercia
c. 1100-unknown

Richard Shakespeare
c. 1512-1561

Abigail Webb Shakespeare
1515-1595

Sir John Alexander Webb, Jr
c. 1467-1526

Margaret Arden
1588-1648

Mary Webb Arden
1512-1550

John Arden
c. 1467-1526

Sir Thomas Arden
c. 1469-1546

Robert Arden
1506-1566

Sir Henry Webb
c. 1510-1544

Grace Arden Webb
1512-1539

Margaret Arden Webb
1538-1608

Alexander Webb
1534-1573

Abigail married Richard, a tenant farmer who grazed his cattle on the lands of Robert Arden. Robert became his brother-in-law.

Sir John, of Odstock, married Margaret—niece to Sir Thomas Arden. His father was Lord Mayor of London and he himself was a knight and an usher in Queen Catherine Parr's Privy court.

Abigail's older sister married Robert Arden of Wilmcote, whose father was her mother's first cousin. They were a younger branch of the family, but still had estates.

Anne Hathaway
c. 1555-1623

William Hart
1565-1616

Joan Shakespeare Hart
1569-1646

John Shakespeare
c. 1532-1601

Mary Arden Shakespeare
1557-1608

William Shakespeare
1564-1616

Shakespeare allowed his sister to live in the family house after his death. Her descendants continue to the present day.

A glove-maker and tradesman, he held various town offices, but fell into debt and was fined for usury. His fortunes rose again with his famous son's.

She was of the gentry, marrying her yeoman first cousin, but both were illiterate. Her "signature" was a running horse, while John's was two glover's compasses.

Ambitious, like his father, Shakespeare divided his time between London and Stratford. At the age of 49 he retired to Stratford, where he died.

26 years old compared to Shakespeare's 18 years, she was several months pregnant when they married. They had three children before he moved to London, leaving her with his parents.

Judith Shakespeare Quiney
1585-1622

William Hart
1600-1639

Lady Elizabeth Bernard
1608-1670

Dr. John Hall
1575-1635

Susanna Shakespeare Hall
1583-1649

Hamnet
1585-1596

Judith lost her twin, Hamnet, at age 11. Her three children died young—two to plague.

Thomas Quiney
1589-1657

Joan's son performed with the King's Men, most noted for playing the character Falstaff. He never married, but a leading actor of the restoration period, Charles Hart, may be his son.

She was the only grandchild Shakespeare knew. She married twice and inherited the family estate, but died childless—the last of Shakespeare's direct descendants.

When she married John, it is believed she was given a substantial dowry from her father, including 105 acres of land. They had one child, Elizabeth.

Catherine the Great

Catherine the Great's reign is considered Russia's Golden Age. She extended Russia's territory, encouraged westernisation, established the first school for women, and supported the Russian Enlightenment—when arts and the sciences flourished. She was even seen as more capable than her husband, the Tsar Peter III. In addition to collecting art, Catherine corresponded with great thinkers like Diderot and Voltaire, and wrote plays and memoirs. The Catherinian Era was not peaceful, however: it began with her husband's assassination. The Epidemic of 1771 caused the Plague Riot in Moscow, where up to 100,000 died of the plague. Still, by the end of Catherine's 34-year reign, Russia had become one of the great powers of Europe.

Crown Jewels

The Imperial Crown of Russia was created for Catherine and used until 1917. It has 4,936 diamonds, arranged in surface patterns. Other gems include pearls, the seven historic stones from the Russian Diamond Collection, and an enormous red spinel (the Balas Ruby), which was brought to Russia in the 1670s by the Russian envoy to China.

The Romanovs

The Romanovs trace back to a member of Russian aristocracy from around 1347, who founded 12 Muscovite noble families. In 1547, Anastasia Romanovna married into the ancient Rurik dynasty. Founded in 862, it lasted to 1610. In 1613, after three years of turmoil, the Romanov dynasty began with Michael I. Russian names use patronyms, so Alexey, son of Mikhail, becomes Alexey Mikhailovitch while Anastasia, daughter of Roman, is Anastasia Romanovna. The title Tsar and Autocrat of All the Russias began with Ivan III the Great, who established Byzantine customs.

Ivan IV the Terrible, House of Rurik
1530-1584

Popular with the commoners, he hated and controlled the nobility and devised a bureaucracy to rule his territories.

Anastasia Romanovna
1530-1560

m

She was chosen to be Ivan IV's consort from hundreds of eligible noble women presented at the Kremlin. She was Michael I's paternal great-aunt.

Feodor Nikitich Romanov
1553-1633

He was the father of the first Romanov tsar and patriarch of Moscow. He reformed the tax structure, established libraries, and reorganized the military.

Michael I of Russia
1596-1645

The Zemsky Sobor (the Russian Parliament) chose him to be tsar at age 16, after none of the Rurik descendants would accept.

Holstein-Gottorp Family

Johanna Elisabeth
1712-1760

m

Christian August
1690-1747

Her father was regent for his nephew, who became Peter III's father. She was unhappy, following her soldier husband to the boring town of Stettin, and resented her daughter Sophia, who was to become empress of Russia.

Tsar Peter III (Karl Peter Ulrich)
1728-1762

A German who spoke little Russian, Peter was unpopular due to his support of Russia's Prussian enemy, Frederick II. Catherine unseated him, and then her supporters immediately assassinated him.

Catherine I (Marta Samuilovna Skavronskaya)
1684-1727

m

The daughter of a Polish-Lithuanian peasant, she eventually became Peter the Great's mistress, and later his wife and successor. She was able to calm Peter's rages and epileptic fits.

Tsar Peter I the Great
1672-1725

He expanded and modernized the empire, changing Russia from a medieval serfdom to a scientific, westernised power. He moved the capital from Moscow to St. Petersburg.

Catherine the Great (Sophie Friederike Auguste von Arnhalt Zerbst)
1729-1796

m

She did not remarry after Peter III's assassination, instead taking a series of lovers—40 in all. Some, like Potemkin, were given high posts of honor. All received estates and wealth as pensions.

Nicholas II
1848-1917

He was forced to give up the throne after the February Revolution of 1917. Months later, he and his family were executed by the Bolshevik party.

Duke Charles Frederick of Schleswig-Holstein-Gottorp
1700-1739

m

Charles and Anna's marriage was seen as politically useful. Anna died upon the birth of their son, who later became tsar.

Anna Petrovna Romanova
1708-1728

Beautiful, educated, refined, and gentle, she was miserable in her short marriage of policy to the drunken Duke Charles Frederick.

Marie Antoinette

"Did Queen Marie Antoinette's extravagance cause the French Revolution? It's a complicated question. When the Hapsburg princess married Louis XVI, France was almost bankrupt. The young queen loved parties and expensive clothes, but so did others. When she attempted serious political action, she became the target of plots and gossip. For example, she reportedly heard the peasants could not afford bread and replied,

"Then let them eat cake!" When King Louis tried to introduce tax changes to relieve the national debt, the people of France revolted. Marie sought other countries' aid, and when that was unsuccessful, they tried to escape. In 1793, the king and Marie were separately tried and executed. The monarchy was at an end. The charming queen died as a traitor to France...But was she?

The French Court

"I put on my rouge and wash my hands before the whole world," the 17-year-old queen complained to her mother. In the French court, close to 50 ladies-in-waiting (members of the nobility), attended her at all ceremonies, including getting dressed for the day.

The Reign of Terror and "Saint" Guillotine

The guillotine was invented to "humanely" behead criminals. It became a symbol of The Terror—the darkest stretch of the French Revolution. This was a year-long period when 16,594 "traitors" were executed. The Terror ended when the Republic's leader, Robespierre, was executed, but the guillotine remained in use.

The Hapsburgs and Bourbons

The marriage of Marie Antoinette and Louis XVI connected the houses of Hapsburg and Bourbon. The Hapsburgs ruled the Holy Roman Empire from 1438-1740 and provided kings for most European courts. In the 16th century, the family divided. Maria Theresa of Austria (Marie Antoinette's mother) married Francis Stephen of Lorraine: the Hapsburg monarchy became the House of Hapsburg-Lorraine. During the French Revolution, when the king and queen became mere citizens, they were called Louis and Marie Capet.

HOUSE OF HAPSBURG

Ferdinand III
1608-1657

He headed the Imperial Army during the Thirty Years' War. While most of his reign was spent conducting wars and treaties, he was also a talented composer of music.

Charles VI, Holy Roman Emperor
1685-1740

Through the Pragmatic Sanction of 1713, he fought for his inheritance to pass to his daughter, Maria, as his only son had died early. But this later led to her fighting several wars to prove herself as his heiress.

Maria Theresa Walburga Amalia Christina of Austria
1717-1780

She was the only female to rule the Hapsburg Empire, effectively ruling her husband's realms as well. Theirs was a love match, as well as a marriage of policy.

Eleanor Maria Josepha of Austria
1653-1697

She was married twice, first to the king of Poland and then to the Duke of Lorraine. She was Marie Antoinette's great-grandmother.

Francis Stephen of Lorraine
1708-1765

Through Maria Theresa's influence, he became Holy Roman Emperor, as well as King of the Germans. He gave up the territory of the Duchy of Lorraine in exchange for the Grand Duchy of Tuscany.

Henry IV of Navarre
1553-1610

The first Bourbon king, he converted to Catholicism in order to end religious fighting over the crown. Both religions said he was a traitor, and after 12 attempts, he was assassinated.

Marie Antoinette (Maria Antonia Josepha Johanna), Queen Consort of France
1755-1793

Her marriage to Louis XVI was arranged when she was just 10 years old, to cement the Austrian-French alliance after the Seven Years' War.

HOUSE OF BOURBON

Hugh Capet, Count of Paris and King of the Franks
1653-1697

Although he started the French Monarchy, the France of his day had very different boundaries. Paris was the hub of his growing realm.

Louis XIV, Sun King
1638-1715

A great and respected monarch, he fought for territory and centralized power. The nobility was forced to live with him at Versailles, where he could both support and control them.

Louis XVI of France
1754-1793

One cause of the French Revolution was Louis's support of the American War of Independence.

Wolfgang Amadeus Mozart

When he was seven, Mozart proposed to a young Marie Antoinette, or so the story goes. It was his first tour of the courts of Europe, being shown off as a child prodigy. In addition to advancing his reputation, the tour set the pattern for the rest of his life: performing, improvising, composing, working with the best musicians, and traveling in search of posts. His domineering father wanted to keep him in Salzburg in the archbishop's court, but Mozart was restless. He ended up in Vienna. To keep him there, Emperor Joseph II (the "Musical King") gave him a part-time post writing dances for the annual ball.

Composer Extraordinaire

Mozart could write and perform anything. Starting at age five, he composed over 600 pieces before his early death. He debuted his works in places like restaurants, which were cheap to rent. His popularity has never waned, and today he is known as the premier classical composer.

Vienna

Mozart's father was a Baroque-era musician. During that time, the best positions were at court. But Mozart composed in the classical age, the Age of Enlightenment. Commoners wanted music and more concerts used non-court venues. Vienna was the musical center, and Mozart loved the city's intensity and variety.

The Mozart Family

In the 1600s, the Mozarts were farmers near Augsburg, Bavaria. In 1743, Mozart's father left Augsburg and became a musician at the court of the Archbishop of Salzburg. His wife's father, also a skilled musician, had a degree in jurisprudence (theory of law) from Salzburg's Benedictine University.

MOZART

WEBER

Anna Maria Walburga Pertl
1720-1778

Mozart's mother provided a refuge from her children's domineering father, and Mozart loved her deeply.

Johann Georg Leopold Mozart
1719-1787

Starting as a violinist, he rose to be a conductor and composer for the court of the Prince-Archbishop of Salzburg.

Franz Fridolin Weber
1733-1779

The son and brother of musicians, he fell back on music when he lost his bailiff and bookkeeping jobs. In Munich, he was a bassist, prompter, and music copyist.

Cacilia Weber
1727-1793

Maria Anna Walburga Ignatia Mozart 1751-1829

Known as Marianne and nicknamed Nannerl, Mozart's older sister received top billing on the family tours in the early days.

Maria Anna Thekla Mozart
1758-1841

The daughter of Leopold's brother Franz Alois, she met Mozart when she was 19 and he was 21, and the two had a close relationship.

Aloysia Weber Lange
1760-1839

The family followed her singing career to Munich and Vienna, and she was their breadwinner.

Carl Maria Friedrich Ernst von Weber 1786-1826

He was Constanze's first cousin. A musician, composer, and conductor, he is best known as a proponent of the Romantic style.

Wolfgang Amadeus Mozart
1756-1791

Mozart idolized his sister as a child, and they were the only surviving children. The two had a secret language and invented an imaginary kingdom, which they ruled together.

Constanze Weber
1762-1842

Mozart originally wanted to marry Constanze's older sister Aloysia, whom he met in Mannheim's circles. He fell in love with Constanze in Vienna.

Sophie Weber Haibl
1763-1846

Mozart flirted with both Constanze and Sophie, but eventually decided that Sophie was "good-natured but feather-brained."

Maria Josepha Weber Hofer Mayer
1758-1819

She sang the Queen of the Night's soaring soprano aria in the debut of *The Magic Flute* (1791). Her second husband, Sebastian Meier, played Pizarro in the premiere of Beethoven's *Fidelio*.

Desiree Clary

Although young and naïve, Desiree Clary was courted by two of the greatest generals of her time: Napoleon Bonaparte, Emperor of France, and Jean-Baptiste Bernadotte, who became King of Sweden.

In 1794, she was engaged to Napoleon. However, Napoleon soon jilted Desiree for an elegant Revolutionary widow, Josephine de Beauharnais. Desiree was broken-hearted, but by 1798 she was married to Jean-Baptiste Bernadotte, one of Emperor Napoleon's best generals. Bernadotte was later adopted by the childless King Charles XIII of Sweden to become Sweden's Crown Prince. Sadly, Desiree disliked Sweden's cold weather and the court's non-French formality. She went back to Paris and did not return to Sweden until 1823, when her son married her former rival Josephine's granddaughter. The story had come full circle and Sweden had a new royal dynasty.

A "Spoilt" Child?

While Bernadotte and Napoleon were prominent leaders, Desiree was shy, unsophisticated, and politically clueless. As Queen Hedwig of Sweden said, "The Princess is small, not pretty and with no figure whatsoever. Her timidity makes her brusque... a spoilt child...but sweet, kind and compassionate." What a contrast to the fascinating Josephine!

Revolutionary Times

The times were violent. Josephine narrowly escaped the guillotine that claimed her first husband. Napoleon and Bernadotte fought through the French Revolution to the Restoration, attempting world conquest. King Joseph Bonaparte, put in charge by Napoleon, lost Spain in the Peninsular Wars with Britain. Then came the Battle of Waterloo and Napoleon's final exile.

The Bernadotte Family

The Swedish royal family (the House of Bernadotte) is a mixture of backgrounds and a reflection of the times. Desiree's ancestors were wealthy merchants. Bernadotte's ancestors included shepherds, weavers, and lawyers, but he chose the military. Josephine's father was a Martinique plantation owner. Her first husband, General Alexandre de Beauharnais, was guillotined during the Terror as an aristocrat. Their son, Eugene, married Augusta of Bavaria—a descendant of the Vasas, Sweden's previous dynasty. Their daughter, Josefina, then married Oscar I, Desiree's son. Thus, the House of Bernadotte is French, Prussian, and Swedish!

François Clary
1725-1794

Nobile Maria Letizia Buonaparte née Ramolino
1750-1836

Nobile Carlo Maria Buonaparte
1746-1785

King Carl XIV Johan of Sweden (Jean-Baptiste Bernadotte) 1763-1844

Bernardine Eugénie Désirée Clary
1777-1860

Napoleon's mother was strict and no-nonsense and dominated her family. She joined her son in his exile but finished her days in Rome.

At first a Corsican noble and patriot, he became a French diplomat. His gambling and failed businesses left his family penniless.

He was adopted as Sweden's Crown Prince. Napoleon later released him from military service to become king of Sweden, saying, "Go, and let our destinies be accomplished!"

She rose from the merchant class to become Desideria, Queen Consort of Sweden. Napoleon called her Desiree, the name she used ever after.

Marie Julie Clary
1771-1845

Joseph-Napoléon Bonaparte (Giuseppe), King of Spain 1768-1844

King Oscar I (born Joseph François Oscar Bernadotte) 1799-1859

Joséphine of Leuchtenberg or Joséphine de Beauharnais (Joséphine Maximilienne Eugénie Napoléone) 1807-1876

As the wife of Joseph Bonaparte, Julie's fortunes rose and fell with his and his brother's. However, the couple mostly lived apart. In Spain she was called "the Reina Ausente" ("the Absent Queen").

After Napoleon's downfall, the ex-king of Naples and Spain moved to New Jersey, USA. His home, a rendezvous for French ex-pats, was purchased with Spanish plunder.

Only 11 years old when his father became Crown Prince, Oscar learned Swedish (something his mother never did) and was his father's translator.

Married to Oscar I for her connections, it was a happy partnership, both personally and politically.

A Napoleonic Responsibility

Napoleon provided for his family, including in-laws and stepchildren: they all received lucrative positions and marriages. As a sister-in-law, Desiree received her Parisian house and possibly her marriage. When Napoleon divorced Josephine to form a dynasty, she kept her title, plus houses and income.

Eugène Rose de Beauharnais, Duke of Leuchtenberg 1781-1824

Princess Augusta of Bavaria, Duchess of Leuchtenberg 1788-1851

Joséphine de Beauharnais, Empress of France, born Marie-Joséphe Rose Tascher de La Pagerie 1763-1814

Napoléon Bonaparte, Emperor of France 1769-1821

Alexandre de Beauharnais
1760-1794

Napoleon's adopted son, he proved the ablest of Napoleon's appointees. He married Augusta of Bavaria, a descendant of the Vasa line.

She escaped her estranged husband's fate and captivated Napoleon. Although her "use" name was Rose, he preferred the name Josephine.

Considered one of the greatest military commanders in history, he conquered much of Europe in the 19th century. He made himself emperor of France in 1804 but was exiled in 1815.

Maharaja Ranjit Singh

In 1802, the 21-year-old Maharaja Ranjit Singh created the Sikh Empire in northern India's Punjab region. A Jat Sikh, he fought his first battle when he was 10 and never stopped. Religious persecution by the Mughal Empire (1569-1799) had turned Sikhs into fighters who used cavalry and guerrilla tactics, including the highly-skilled "running skirmish."

Hiding in the jungles and Himalayan foothills, they eventually formed quarrelsome bands called Misls, which fought against common enemies (the Mughal, Afghan and Maratha empires). It was the Maharaja who unified them.

A Believer

Sikhism started in Punjab in the 1500s. It reached its height under the Maharaja. Yet, Ranjit also employed Hindus, Muslims, and Europeans. The Sikh faith emphasises cooperation over caste, and does not believe one religion holds the ultimate truth. The empire was organized through Sikh principles and common goals, rather than religion. Since the Maharaja, Sikhism has become the world's ninth-largest religion.

'The Sun Only Has One Eye

Smallpox left the infant Ranjit's left eye blind. In India, blindness meant loss of power, but not for him. Asked which eye was blinded, a follower said the Maharaja was "one-eyed like the Sun" and, due to "the splendor of his single eye," the follower had never dared to look.

The Singh Family

Like the ancient Greeks, families in India trace their descent from gods and legendary patriarchs. We know about the ancient Indo-Aryan tribes through the Hindi psalms of the Rigveda, which was composed during the Bronze Age. Much later, around AD 1500, the Maharaja's ancestors, the Jat tribes, appeared in Punjab. When the Misls formed, over half were Jat Singh.

Sardar Budh Singh
1670-1718

Lord Krishna
c. 3169-3059 BC

Rawal Jaisal
c. 1085-1168

Lali Kaur
c. 1656-1716

— m —

Sardar Naudh Singh
unknown-1752

Originally known as Desu, he was a prosperous farmer as well as a bold warrior. He owned 25 acres of land, where he founded the village of Sukkarchakk, near the holy city of Amritsar.

Sardarni Desan Kaur Sukerchakia
c. 1754-1778

Sada Kaur
c. 1762-1832

In 1730, he joined the Sikh warriors in the jungles. In 1749, while battling Afghan invaders, he was crippled by a shot to the head.

A Yadu descendant, he fulfilled prophecy when he established the fort of Jaisalmer on a sandstone ridge. The 15th-century Jat Sikh kings of Patiala descend from him.

— m —

Sardar Maha Singh
unknown-1792

Tilok Chand Singh, founder of Jind Jat
c. 1611-1687

Sardar Charat Singh
1721-1774

Gajpat Singh, a Jind Jat
1738-1789

A strong ally, she was chief of the Kanhaiya Misl from 1789 to 1821, following the deaths of her husband and father-in-law. She helped in Ranjit's early victories.

He led the Sukerchakia Misl. An able leader and chief of the Chattha Jat Tribe, he died when Ranjit was 12. His wife, a Jind Jat, became regent.

— m —

Raj Kaur Singh
c. 1743

Maharani Mehtab Kaur
c. 1782-1813

In his youth, he fought against Ahmad Shah Abdali (founder of Afghanistan). He and 150 horsemen left the Singhpuria Misl to form the Sukerchakia Misl.

— m —

Maharaja Ranjit Singh
1780-1839

Maharaja Duleep Singh
1838-1893

Rani Jindan (Maharandi Jind Kaur)
1817-1863

She was the senior wife, marrying Ranjit when she was 15. Her son, Maharaja Sher Singh, ruled the Sikh Empire from 1841 to 1843, when he was assassinated.

Bambjon Muller
1848-1918

— m —

— m —

Prince Victor Albert Jay Duleep Singh
1866-1918

Named Maharaja at age five, he was removed from power at age 10, after the Second Anglo-Sikh War. He spent the rest of his life under the control of his British "handlers."

Ranjit's youngest wife served as regent from 1843 to 1846. When the British won the First Anglo-Sikh War, she was imprisoned and exiled. She did not see her son for 13 years.

His 20 wives were Sikh, Hindu and Muslim. He spent his teens fighting the Afghans, assuming leadership of the Misl at age 18. He became Maharaja three years later.

Mary Shelley

Mary Godwin Shelley, the creator of *Frankenstein*, is now one of the world's best-loved gothic novelists. However, when she first met the Romantic poet, Percy Bysshe Shelley, he was the famous one. He was also married, but fell in love with Mary—his intellectual equal. The couple eloped to Europe when she was 16 and he 22. They returned after just six weeks, penniless, to be rejected by both their families. Their years together were spent in Italy, writing and associating with Lord Byron and other Romantics. Sadly, Percy died at age 29, when his sailboat capsized. Mary, a widow at 24, returned to England, where she focused on her husband's poetic legacy. Thus, her own works—other than the hugely popular *Frankenstein*—were all but forgotten until the 1970s.

A Ghost-Writing Contest

One rainy Swiss summer, Lord Byron's friends were gathered by the fire telling ghost stories. Everyone was challenged to write one. Mary's central image of a man-creature came a few nights later, in a waking dream. Her written story expanded into the great gothic novel Frankenstein.

The Godwin-Shelleys

Mary was the daughter of the radical philosopher William Godwin, who described her as "singularly bold, somewhat imperious, and active of mind." Her mother, who died days after her birth, was the famous defender of women's rights, Mary Wollstonecraft. Mary grew up with five semi-related siblings in Godwin's unconventional but intellectually electric household, so was surprised when she was rejected by her father for eloping in a similarly unconventional manner.

Mary Jane Vial Clairmont
1768-1841

m

Little is known about her life before her marriage to William. They were married twice on the same day, in 1801, and it is believed the second ceremony was to protect against the first being voided.

William Godwin
1756-1836

m

A political philosopher, Mary Shelley's father is also the father of anarchy. He wrote constantly, in many genres. The candid memoir of his wife shocked his Victorian readers.

Mary Wollstonecraft
1759-1797

m

She died at Mary's birth. Her notorious lifestyle outweighed her powerful works of feminist philosophy and social criticism. Today both her life and work are inspiring.

Gilbert Imlay
1754-1828

He met Wollstonecraft during the French Revolution. She was making notes; he was running the blockade. He deserted his lover and their child in Paris.

William Godwin, Jr.
1768-1841

Charles Clairmont
1768-1841

Frances "Fanny" Imlay Wollstonecraft Godwin 1794-1816

Jane Clairmont
1768-1841

Mary Wollstonecraft Godwin Shelley.
1797-1851

Lord Byron
1768-1841

m

Mary's stepsister was included in the elopement because she spoke French. Later she had Lord Byron's child, Allegra, who died of typhus aged five.

Because she lost three children and her husband at an early age, her later years were focused on her only remaining child.

Percy Bysshe Shelley.
1792-1822

m

A great Romantic lyrical poet, he was also a radical and strongly influenced by William Godwin's writings. He met Mary after his entrance into Godwin's circle.

When Mary and Claire (Jane) fled with Percy, Mary's half sister Fanny was devastated to be left behind. Isolated, she committed suicide two years later.

Harriet Shelley
1797-1851

m

Harriet married Percy just after her sixteenth birthday. They later became estranged and she grew increasingly unhappy. In 1816, she drowned herself.

Allegra Byron
1817-1822

Charles Shelley
1797-1851

Ianthe Shelley
1797-1851

Lost in Literature

The Godwin household had a number of distinguished guests during Shelley's childhood, including Samuel Taylor Coleridge and William Wordsworth. While Shelley didn't have a formal education, she did make great use of her father's extensive library. She could often be found reading, sometimes by her mother's grave. She also liked to daydream, escaping from her often challenging home life into her imagination.

Sir Percy Florence Shelley, 3rd Baronet 1819-89

He was named after the city of his birth, Florence. He and his wife revered his parents, and Mary lived with them until her death.

Clara Shelley
1815-1815

William Shelley
1816-1819

Clara Everina Shelley
1817-1818

Abraham Lincoln

The sixteenth US president, Abraham Lincoln, was a storyteller known for his integrity and "extraordinary sweetness." Yet, despite his humor and compassion, he was a staunch commander-in-chief during the country's devastating Civil War. The young Lincoln endured poverty and gruelling work on frontier farms. Ambitious, he left, working odd jobs while teaching himself law. He then entered Illinois politics, campaigning for a modern world without slavery.

In 1860, Lincoln was elected US president. Seven Southern slave-owning states reacted by forming the Confederate States of America. The Civil War began shortly thereafter. Lincoln oversaw the war effort, defeating the South and keeping the country united. In 1863, he signed the Emancipation Proclamation. This was an order to free slaves—and although not all were immediately freed, it did lead the way to their freedom two years later.

Assassination

On April 14, 1865, President Lincoln was attending a play at the Ford Theatre in Washington, DC, when he was shot in the head by John Wilkes Booth. Booth was angry that the southern states were losing in the War and reportedly shouted, "The South is avenged!" when he fired the gun.

Famous Speech

The Gettysburg Address, barely two minutes long, is one of the most famous speeches in American history. It was given by Lincoln on November 19, 1863, at the dedication of the National Cemetery at Gettysburg, Pennsylvania. In the speech he references the ideals and principles of equality, freedom, and democracy.

The Lincoln Family

While most of Lincoln's ancestors were English, some came from France and the Netherlands. His father's grandmother descended from King Edward I. A French ancestor joined William the Conqueror in his 1066 invasion of England, and Dutch ancestors emigrated to New York. Lincoln's ancestors became prosperous land-owners, known for their integrity and public service. They combined farming with trades such as weaving. Many held the Puritan or Quaker beliefs that would later influence Abraham's views on slavery.

Lucy Hanks Sparrow
1767–1783

Capt. Abraham Lincoln
1744–1786
m
Bathseba Herring
1742–1836

Nancy Hanks Lincoln
c. 1784–1818
m
Thomas Lincoln
1778–1851

Edward Baker Lincoln
1846–1850

Self-educated, she taught Lincoln from the Bible. He claimed, "all that I am or hope ever to be I get from my mother." Her death came from milk contaminated by cows eating poisonous white snakeroot.

Complicated land titles and issues with slavery caused Thomas to leave Kentucky for Indiana. He was a strict disciplinarian who caned his son.

Eddie may have inherited a genetic disorder. His early death was listed as "chronic consumption," which covered many wasting diseases of the time.

Abraham Lincoln
1809–1865

Mary Ann Todd Lincoln
1818–1882

William Wallace "Willie" Lincoln
1850–1862

Thomas "Tad" Lincoln III
1853–1871

She was holding Lincoln's hand when he was shot. Chronic ill-health and personal tragedies affected the mental health of this educated daughter of slave-owners.

Lincoln could not wait to leave his father, who hired him out to other farmers and did not value education.

After Willie's death from typhoid, Lincoln repeatedly wept in private, while Mary took to her bed for three weeks and needed a nurse afterward.

Nicknamed "Tad" because he was as "wriggly as a tadpole," he interrupted White House meetings and charged visitors to see his father.

Robert Todd Lincoln
1843–1926
m
Mary Eunice Harlan
1846–1937

Jessie Harlan Lincoln
1875–1948

Mary Lincoln "Peggy" Beckwith
1898–1975

Robert Todd Lincoln Beckwith
1904–1985

Mary Todd "Mamie" Lincoln Isham
1869–1938

Abraham "Jack" Lincoln II
1873–1890

Robert and Lincoln were not close: his childhood memory is of Lincoln packing his saddlebags for political meetings.

Warren Wallace Beckwith
1874–1955
m

She eloped with fellow student Beckwith, who became a minor league baseball player. Jessie's financial trust was larger than her sister's because she was often financially irresponsible.

Smart and eccentric, she learned to fly and managed the family farm during and after the First World War.

He was Lincoln's last direct descendant, a "gentleman farmer of independent means."

Charles Dickens

From the Christmastime icon Ebenezer Scrooge to the semi-autobiographical Oliver Twist, Charles Dickens created some of the most memorable characters of English literature. Forced to leave school at age 15, within a year he found himself a fully-fledged court reporter, and within six years he was a popular freelance journalist and novelist, lecturing and conducting well-paid readings. On one tour of America it is said that he earned what would today be $3 million! Although Dickens's earlier writings were humorous, later books and lectures centered around social issues of the day, such as slavery, poverty, and debtor's prisons, social ills and poor working conditions. His boyhood memories provided many details. As his epitaph says: "He was a sympathizer to the poor, the suffering, and the oppressed; and by his death, one of England's greatest writers is lost to the world."

No Spoilers, Please!

In Dickens's time, most books were first published in weekly or monthly installments in the newspapers. While many stories were hardly great literature, Dickens's hugely popular *Pickwick Papers* proved that serials could be both financially successful and well-written. The Victorian reader thus awaited each installment with the same eagerness today's TV watchers feel.

Stoney Broke and in the Clink

It was a crime to be poor. When Charles Dickens was 12, his family was imprisoned for his father's debts. Charles, the eldest son, had to work at a bootblack factory. A famous debtors' prison was the Clink, on Stoney Street. So, in slang terms, prisoners were "in the clink" because they were "stoney broke."

The Dickens Family

Dickens's paternal grandparents were servants of John Crewe, a wealthy landowner with estates in Cheshire and a house in Mayfair; there he often entertained prominent artists and writers. One of the guests, playwright Richard Brinsley Sheridan, got John Dickens his navy office job, which raised him from the servant class. Dickens's Scottish in-laws were of higher social standing, as they were publishers and writers with prominent literary connections.

DICKENS FAMILY

HOGARTH FAMILY

Charles Barrow
1759-1826

He was the Chief Conductor of Monies at Somerset House in London.

Mary Culliford
1771-1851

m

William Dickens
1716-1785

He became a steward for Lord Crewe in Cheshire, where he met Elizabeth.

Elizabeth Ball
c. 1745-1824

m

Became housekeeper for the Crewes when she married William Dickens.

George Thomson
1757-1851

A music publisher, known for editing Scottish folk songs to semi-classical settings.

Mary C. Barrow
1789-1863

In Charles's words, Mary was "an amazing woman."

John Dickens
1785-1851

m

Inspiration for the character Mr. Micawber, Charles called him "a jovial opportunist with no money sense."

George Hogarth
1783-1870

A talented cellist and journalist, he became co-owner of the Edinburgh Weekly Journal.

Georgiana Thomson
1793-1863

m

Her childhood balanced parties with schooling. George's musical interests brought him close to Georgina's family.

Fanny Dickens
1810-1848

Although money was tight, she was a student at the expensive Royal Academy of Music.

Charles Dickens
1812-1870

From the age of 12, he became the head of the family, supporting his mother and sisters financially.

Catherine Hogarth
1815-1879

m

Her literary connections and unaffected manners attracted Dickens.

Mary Hogarth
1819-1827

Beautiful and gentle, she regularly lived with the couple in London and died in Charles Dickens's arms.

Georgina Hogarth
1827-1917

In her teens she joined the Dickens family, serving as companion and housekeeper when the Dickenses separated.

Ada Lovelace

The world's first computer programmer, Ada Lovelace, read about Charles Babbage's Analytical Engine invention in the 1830s and went on to create the world's first computer code. As a wealthy noblewoman, Ada was tutored at home. Her lessons focused on mathematics and science, in a bid to guard her against the influence of her estranged poet father, Lord Byron.

Because of her brilliance and family connections, she had access to the great thinkers of the day, including Babbage, a mathematician. Ada was the first to think that this machine could do more than add and subtract: it could be a machine that converted images, language and music to numbers. Today, Ada is considered to be the Mother of Modern Computing.

Could the Analytical Engine Work?

Ada died young and Babbage had financial difficulties, so they never built their machine. However, in 1991, the London Science Museum completed the Difference Engine No.2, built to Babbage's specifications. Once a few bugs were removed, it worked!

Poetic Science

Ada was brought up by two very strong women—her mother and her grandmother. Her mother had separated from the mentally unstable poet Lord Byron when Ada was a month old. Loving math and science herself, and fearing the effect of the more emotional arts like poetry, she insisted that Ada learn science in addition to the socially necessary skills of music and French. Later, Ada would move from the strict logic of math to make her poetic and visionary leaps into the world of computing.

The Lovelace Family

Ada's aristocratic family was characterized by strong wealthy women who married spendthrift, flamboyant, and mentally unstable men. Her father, Lord Byron, married into the wealth of the Lovelace family and is widely regarded as a brilliant poet and the leader of the Romantic movement in literature.

BYRON FAMILY

NOEL FAMILY

Through Edward Noel, Ada can trace her lineage back to King Edward III.

MILBANKE FAMILY

William 5th Lord Byron
1722-1798

He was commonly called "the Wicked Lord" after he killed his cousin.

Vice Admiral Byron
1723-1786

He was also known as "Foulweather Jack" due to his frequent encounters with storms at sea.

Sophia Trevanian
1727-1790

She married Foulweather Jack, by whom she had two sons and seven daughters.

King Edward III

Edward Noel 1st Viscount
1715-1774

Edward Noel's descendants were the source of Ada's fortune.

William Byron
1722-1798   m   *Lady Darcy*

Juliana Byron
1753-1788

Captain Byron
1756-1791

An army officer nicknamed "Mad Jack," he changed his last name to Gordon.

Catherine Gordon
1770-1811

Sir Ralph
1747-1825

A politician, he took his wife's name in order to inherit her estate.

Frances Byron

Judith Noel
1751-1822

Colonel Leigh
1715-1774   m

Augusta Leigh
1783-1851

She was George Byron's half sister by his father's first wife. Her daughter was rumored to be Lord Byron's.

George Gordon 6th Lord Byron
1788-1824

One of Britain's most revered poets, Lord Byron was "mad and bad."

Lady Melbourne
1751-1818

She was a hostess for the Whig political party, who became Lord Byron's confidante during his affair.

Complicated Relationships

Ada's mother's aunt, Lady Melbourne, was Lord Byron's friend and the mother-in-law of Byron's mistress, Lady Caroline Lamb. Lord Byron was also associated with his half sister, Augusta Leigh, who married their paternal aunt's son, George Leigh, and whose daughter, Elizabeth Medora, was possibly Ada's half sister. Ada supported Augusta and Elizabeth for many years.

m   *Anne Wentworth*
1792-1860

Brought up with strict morals, she became obsessed with Lord Byron.

Ada Lovelace, 1815-1852

Music was a lifelong interest of Ada's. She wrote extensively to her mother of the work she was doing in composing music based on numbers—an application she envisioned for the Analytic Engine. She married William King-Noel and had three children before her untimely death.

Charlotte Brontë

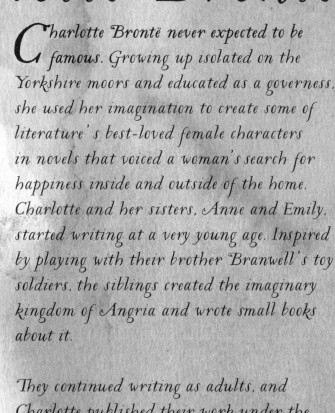

Charlotte Brontë never expected to be famous. Growing up isolated on the Yorkshire moors and educated as a governess, she used her imagination to create some of literature's best-loved female characters in novels that voiced a woman's search for happiness inside and outside of the home. Charlotte and her sisters, Anne and Emily, started writing at a very young age. Inspired by playing with their brother Branwell's toy soldiers, the siblings created the imaginary kingdom of Angria and wrote small books about it.

They continued writing as adults, and Charlotte published their work under the gender-neutral pseudonyms of Currer, Acton, and Ellis Bell (using their real initials). After the deaths of Anne and Emily, Charlotte continued to write, and soon married her father's curate, Arthur Bell Nicholls. Her works, *Jane Eyre*, *The Professor*, and *Villette*, are today considered masterpieces.

The Missing Face

If you visit London's National Portrait Gallery, you can find a creased canvas—an oil painting of the three Brontë sisters, Anne, Emily, and Charlotte—painted by their brother, Branwell. A pillar separates Charlotte from her sisters, but if you look closely at that pillar, you can see signs of another face, that of the 17-year-old artist. The portrait was hidden until 1914, when it was found on top of a cupboard in the cottage of Arthur Bell Nicholls, Charlotte's husband. We still do not know why Branwell took himself out of the picture.

The Power of the Pen

In writing *Jane Eyre*, Charlotte drew from events in her own life, such as the early loss of her mother. Her character's escape was marriage, but Charlotte's was literature. After *Jane Eyre*'s instant success, she claimed authorship and published books in her own name.

The Brontë Family

The original Brontë surname was variously spelled Prunty, Brunty, and Bruntee. Rumor has it that Charlotte's father Patrick changed the spelling in honor of Lord Nelson, the First Duke of Brontë. Charlotte's maternal grandfather, Thomas Branwell, came from a socially and politically prominent family in Penzance, Cornwall. Thomas inherited the family business and was the town butcher, later becoming a merchant and property owner. This contrasts with the peasant background of the Brunty family.

Hugh Brunty 1755–c.1808

Patrick Brontë's adoptive grandfather was the inspiration for *Wuthering Heights's* Heathcliff.

Patrick Brontë 1777–1861

Patrick's parents were semi-illiterate, but he attended Cambridge University and became a Church of England priest.

Maria Brontë 1814–1825

The eldest child, she was the model for *Jane Eyre's* Helen Burns.

Arthur Bell Nicholls 1819–1906

Patrick Brontë's curate and Charlotte's husband.

Eleanor "Alice" McClory 1776–c.1822

Her family's cottage in County Down can be seen on the Brontë Homeland Drive.

Maria Branwell 1783–1821

Maria wrote an unpublished essay, *The Advantages of Poverty in Religious Concerns*, but had little experience of poverty herself.

Elizabeth Brontë 1815–1825

Unlike her governess sisters, she was being schooled to be a housekeeper before she caught tuberculosis.

Charlotte Brontë 1816–1855

Charlotte died soon after her marriage to Arthur, from either pneumonia, tuberculosis or complications during pregnancy.

Thomas Branwell 1746–1808

He rose in business to be elected to the town council of Penzance, his greatest ambition.

Patrick Branwell Brontë 1817–1848

Talented and troubled, the only son of the family could not hold down a job and became an alcoholic and opium addict.

Emily Jane Brontë 1818–1848

Emily's masterpiece, *Wuthering Heights*, is a gothic novel of love and brutality, betrayal and revenge.

Anne Carne 1744–1809

Anne Carne Branwell had 12 children in 20 years—so the family needed to purchase multiple houses in old Penzance.

Elizabeth ("Aunt") Branwell 1776–1842

Caring for Maria's children after Maria's early death, "Aunt" Branwell's Cornish background was used in Emily's novel.

Anne Brontë 1820–1849

Born shortly before her mother's death, she died a year after her sister Emily and brother, Patrick.

Ned Kelly

Ned Kelly could be described as Australia's very own Robin Hood. Notorious for stealing from the wealthy white colonialists settling on the land, some see him as a folk hero, while others simply see him as a criminal. First sent to jail at the age of 14 for stealing a horse, he and his gang had many run-ins with the law, most notably a shoot-out that resulted in him killing three police officers. They committed further offenses, demanding justice for their family and the poor. Outlawed, a bounty of £2,000 ($375,000 today) was offered for the Gang's capture, dead or alive. On July 5, 1880, the final Siege at Glenrowan took place. Only Ned survived. He was executed in November of that year, despite rallies and petitions for his freedom.

The Kelly Family

In Ned Kelly's day, over a fourth of Victoria's residents were originally Irish tenant farmers, who had escaped the Potato Famine. Ned's father, "Red," was transported to Australia with a seven-year sentence for stealing two pigs, whereas his mother, Ellen, belonged to a family of free settlers. Five of Red's siblings also settled in Victoria. The Quinn, Lloyd, and Kelly clans intermarried and drew police attention for their association with stock thieves. After the Kelly Gang was destroyed, the remaining family members settled into respectable life, keeping quiet about the past until 130 years later—when they gathered to re-bury Ned according to Catholic rites, next to his mom.

James Thomas Quinn *1803-1869* — m — **Mary Anne McClusky** *1809-1894*

Thomas Kelly *1800-1860* — m — **Mary Cody** *c. 1798*

John Lloyd *1825-1879* — m

Catherine Lloyd (Quinn) *1833-1894*

Ellen (Quinn) Kelly *1832-1923* — m — **John "Red" Kelly** *1820-1866*

Bridget Lloyd *1855-1884*

Isaiah Wright *c. 1849*

Her son, Thomas, was Margaret's second common-law husband. Her daughter Bridget married Kelly Gang supporter Isaiah Wright.

Imprisoned after an incident with a constable named Fitzpatrick, she told Ned to "die like a Kelly." She outlived seven of her 12 children.

After receiving his Certificate of Freedom, Red met Ellen while working on her father's land. Ellen was 18 and he was 30.

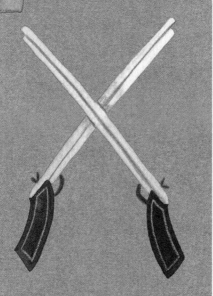

Ned Kelly *c. 1854-1880*

"Kate" Catherine Ada Kelly *1857-1896*

William Henry Foster *1845-1920*

Thomas Peter Lloyd *1857-1927*

Margaret Mildred Lloyd (Kelly) *1857-1896*

Rachel Hart *1866-1959* — m

Often said to have been the fifth member of the Kelly Gang, he lived in a common-law marriage with Margaret after she separated from William.

m

While her mother and husband were in jail and her brothers hiding in the bush, Margaret farmed the land, raised the family, and supported the outlaws.

In the Siege of Glenrowan, Ned wore clumsy armor for his final shoot-out with the police. The police officers involved in his capture kept parts of it as souvenirs.

A constable named Fitzpatrick made a pass at 15-year-old Kate at the Kelley homestead. The resulting violence led to their mother's arrest and the outbreak of the Kelly Gang.

m

William Skillion *c. 1853*

James (Jim) Kelly *1859-1946*

Daniel "Dan" Kelly *1861-1880*

Along with Ellen Kelly, he was jailed for six years after the incident at their home between Constable Fitzpatrick and Kate—even though he was not there.

Jim was convicted of stock theft. Afterward, he helped raise his siblings' children. He became reclusive, avoiding Kelly Gang researchers.

One fourth of the Kelly Gang, Dan helped his brother rob banks and take over whole towns. He was killed during the Siege of Glenrowan.

Women at War?

Annie believed women could shoot and still be ladies, so in later years she began teaching. During the First World War, she offered to train a women's regiment and teach marksmanship to the regular army. But women's roles were still restricted. Instead she gave demonstrations to raise money for the Red Cross.

Immigrant Families

Although they toured with the Wild West show, neither Annie Oakley nor her husband, Frank Butler, were Westerners. The Butlers were Irish immigrants, leaving the country for city jobs. They arrived in 1850 when Frank was 13.

Annie Oakley

A sharpshooting star who performed for Queen Victoria, Annie Oakley started life in rural Ohio, US, as humble Phoebe Anne Mosey. When she was six years old, her father died, leaving his large family broke. For two years, young Annie was bound as a servant to a cruel couple she called "the wolves." From an early age, she had taught herself to use her father's rifle, so when she returned to her family, she was able to support them through hunting. At 17, her fame as a marksman led to a famous shooting match with touring sharpshooter Frank Butler—which she won. She also won Frank's heart. Soon they were married and performing with Buffalo Bill's Wild West show throughout Europe and the US. The shy 5-foot girl became a star, known for her poise and ladylike demeanor, as well as her skill with a rifle. After she stopped touring, she continued to fight for a women's right to compete in a man's arena.

The Mosey Family

Annie's family came from Pennsylvania in the US. Settled by religious Quakers, the state was also home to the German Baptists, who were Annie's maternal ancestors. After the Revolutionary War, many moved West, seeking cheaper land. Annie's parents would follow that migration to Ohio, after their Pennsylvania tavern burned down. Her nonviolent background did not prevent her from using her sharpshooting skills to feed the family and build a career.

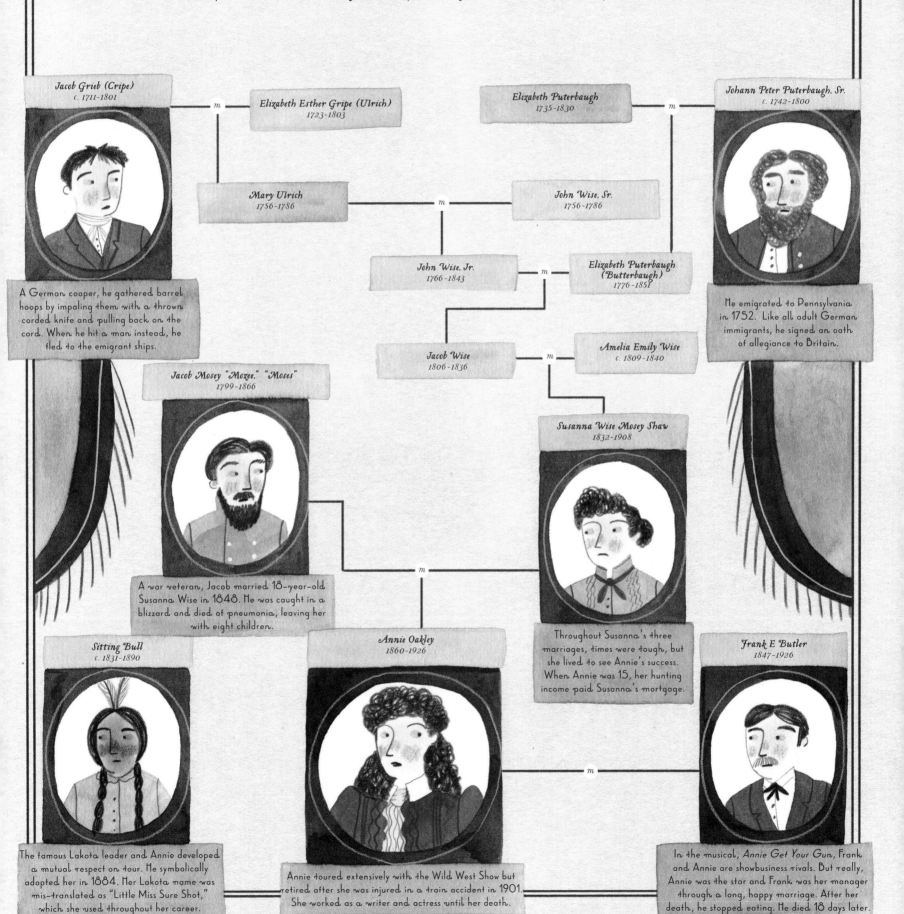

Jacob Grieb (Cripe)
c. 1711–1801

m

Elizabeth Esther Gripe (Ulrich)
1723–1803

Elizabeth Puterbaugh
1735–1830

m

Johann Peter Puterbaugh, Sr.
c. 1742–1800

Mary Ulrich
1756–1786

m

John Wise, Sr.
1756–1786

A German cooper, he gathered barrel hoops by impaling them with a thrown corded knife and pulling back on the cord. When he hit a man instead, he fled to the emigrant ships.

John Wise, Jr.
1766–1843

m

Elizabeth Puterbaugh (Butterbaugh)
1776–1851

He emigrated to Pennsylvania in 1752. Like all adult German immigrants, he signed an oath of allegiance to Britain.

Jacob Wise
1806–1836

m

Amelia Emily Wise
c. 1809–1840

Jacob Mosey "Mozee," "Moses"
1799–1866

Susanna Wise Mosey Shaw
1832–1908

A war veteran, Jacob married 18-year-old Susanna Wise in 1848. He was caught in a blizzard and died of pneumonia, leaving her with eight children.

m

Sitting Bull
c. 1831–1890

Annie Oakley
1860–1926

Throughout Susanna's three marriages, times were tough, but she lived to see Annie's success. When Annie was 15, her hunting income paid Susanna's mortgage.

Frank E Butler
1847–1926

m

The famous Lakota leader and Annie developed a mutual respect on tour. He symbolically adopted her in 1884. Her Lakota name was mis-translated as "Little Miss Sure Shot," which she used throughout her career.

Annie toured extensively with the Wild West Show but retired after she was injured in a train accident in 1901. She worked as a writer and actress until her death.

In the musical, *Annie Get Your Gun*, Frank and Annie are showbusiness rivals. But really, Annie was the star and Frank was her manager through a long, happy marriage. After her death, he stopped eating. He died 18 days later.

Henry Ford

Henry's interests were always mechanical. At age 12, he had a machine shop. At age 16, he became a machinist. Even as a farmer, he focused on the machines. Regardless of his job, he continued to refine and market his automobiles. Finally, in 1908, Ford Motor Company began producing the "Model T." By 1920, it accounted for over half of America's cars.

He was able to mass-produce cheaper cars, all painted black for quicker drying time. By also doubling wages and giving employees leisure time, he increased productivity and boosted the local economy.

He revolutionized the car industry, empowering the workforce and turning a luxury into a necessity.

The Ford Family

In the 1700s, England established plantations in Ireland. Ancestor Thomas Ford's family emigrated from Somerset in England to Cork, becoming tenant farmers. In 1832, Samuel and George Ford emigrated to the Americas, seeking their own land. Henry's grandfather, John Ford, joined them in 1847, fleeing the Potato Famine of Ireland. Not wanting to forget his Irish roots, Henry Ford established his first overseas company in Cork. Today, a stainless-steel sculpture of a Model T sits in the small Irish village of Ballinascarthy—a symbol of Henry's ancestry.

Patrick O'Hearn
1798–1882

Margaret Steven O'Hearn
1786–1870

Thomas Ford
c. 1700

Harvey S. Firestone
1868–1938

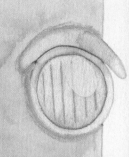

William Ford
1775–1818
— m —
Rebecca Jennings
1776–1851

Edsel Bryant Ford
1893–1943

Eleanor Lowthian Clay
1896–1976

Samuel Ford
1792–1842

John Ford
1799–1862
— m —
Thomasine "Tamsen" Smith
1803–1847

George Ford
1810–1864

He went missing from the British Army in Quebec, moving to Detroit. He and his wife adopted their Belgian neighbor's three-year-old orphan.

William Ford
1826–1905

m

Edsel's innovations, like the Model A, often met Henry's resistance. The stress of producing enough B-24 bombers in the Second World War may have led to his early death.

Edsel courted Eleanor for five years. They liked to help others and donated substantially to the Denver Institute of Art. Edsel commissioned the famous Diego Rivera murals.

Mary Litogot Ford
1839–1876

An Irish farmer and carpenter, he was 21 when the family emigrated. He was called William Ford South, because his cousin, William Ford North, lived across the road.

Henry Ford II
1917–1987

Anne McDonnell
1919–1996

Benson Ford
1919–1978

Edith McNaughton
1920–1980

William met Henry's mother while working on the O'Hearn farm. Ford was devastated by her death. He said it wasn't the farm but "the mother on the farm" he loved.

Henry Ford
1863–1947

Though inexperienced, in 1945 Henry Ford II took over from his grandfather. With him at the helm, company fortunes fluctuated from good to bad.

Quiet and affable, Benson was named Head of the Lincoln-Mercury Division and was also chairman of Henry Ford Hospital.

Clara Jane Bryant
1866–1950

m

Although born to farm, he built his first car in 1896. He then built an automobile empire and founded a family business. Even in retirement, he remained in charge.

Josephine Ford
1823–2005

Walter Buhl Ford II
1920–1991

William Clay Ford
1925–2014

Martha Parke Firestone
1925

Henry called his ever-supportive wife "the believer." Still, when strikes closed factories, she said she'd leave him if he didn't back their son and sign the union contracts.

She donated millions in art and money to the Denver Institute of Art, including a Van Gogh painting. Her youngest son joined the Hare Krishna sect.

As grandchildren of empire builders, their wedding was an Event. A Ford executive, he is best known as owner of the Detroit Lions. His son became the next generation's company president.

Laura Ingalls Wilder

As Laura Ingalls danced to her father's fiddle, listened to his stories and "saw out loud" for her blind sister, she did not know that she was gathering material for what would be the beloved Little House books. She was a pioneer girl, born in 1867. Her family followed Pa's "itchy foot," finally homesteading in DeSmet, South Dakota, US.

There Laura met and married Almanzo Wilder, and the young couple also homesteaded. Crop failures and other disasters then sent them traveling to better fortune in Mansfield, Missouri. Laura added to the family income by writing magazine columns, and in the 1920s, she wrote an autobiography which became *Little House in the Big Woods*—the first of the Little House books. An equally-beloved TV series would later evolve. The stories touch on hardships such as grasshopper plagues, blizzards, isolation, and illness. However, Laura's books mainly celebrate the dauntless and ingenious pioneer spirit.

Hard Work

When the farm did not produce, other jobs had to fill in. Pa called himself a carpenter, while Laura claimed he was "a hunter and trapper, a musician and poet." He was also a shopkeeper and bookkeeper. Laura and her sisters sewed, taught school, and wrote.

Lost Arts

The Little House books are rich with details of tasks like making cheese, butter, candles, straw hats, and bullets. They tell of butchering, stacking hay, breaking the sod, making doughnuts, and weaving. Laura's books are a manual for the lost arts of a vanished way of life.

The Ingalls Family

Laura and Almanzo's families lived through profound national changes: the growth of the railroads, the settlement of the West, and the resettlement of Native Americans. One uncle fought in the Civil War, another panned for gold. For a few months, Laura's Pa worked for the railroad, being hired by his sister's husband as a bookkeeper. Most of their families filed homestead claims—single women included.

INGALLS FAMILY

Lansford Whiting Ingalls
1812-1896

Laura Colby Ingalls
1810-1893

Laura's paternal grandparents lived 13 miles north of the *Big Woods* house. Grandma danced the jig at the sugaring-off dance.

Earlier Migrations

Wanderlust was not new to the families. A Wilder ancestor fought in the Crusades. All families had Puritan immigrant ancestors, with an Ingalls ancestor traveling on the *Mayflower* ship to the New World. Through him, Laura can claim a relationship to US President Franklin Delano Roosevelt.

QUINER FAMILY

Charlotte Quiner/Holbrook (Tucker)
1809-1884

When Ma was 10, her mother married Frederick Holbrook. The Aunt Lotty mentioned in the *Big Woods* is their child. Ma's father drowned in 1844, while on a trading trip.

Laura Ladocia "Docia" Ingalls Forbes
1845-1918

Polly Melona Ingalls
1840-1887

Henry Odin Quiner
1835-1886

Thomas Quiner
1844-1903

Charles Philip Ingalls
1836-1902

Caroline Lake (Quiner) Ingalls
1839-1924

Ruby Celestia Card Ingalls
1855-1881

Eliza Ann Quiner
1842-1931

Peter Riley Ingalls
1833-1900

Henry Odin Quiner married Polly Melona Ingall in 1859. Henry and Pa shared work in the *Big Woods* book.

Described as a quiet gentle man, Uncle Tom prospected for gold in the Black Hills and died in a logging accident, drowning in the Columbia River.

Laura describes her Pa as a fiddler and storyteller; a principled man with great enthusiasms and even greater wanderlust.

Laura's Ma was a schoolteacher at 16. Laura stresses Ma's desire to raise educated, ladylike daughters, despite their rustic pioneer life.

Peter married Eliza in 1861. They come to spend Christmas with double cousins Alice, Ella, and Peter in the *Big Woods* book and traveled with Laura's family to Minnesota.

m

**Laura Elizabeth Ingalls Wilder,
"Mama Bess" 1867-1957**

Almanzo "Manly" James Wilder
1857-1949

Caroline "Carrie" Swanzey (Ingalls) 1870-1946

Grace Pearl Dow (Ingalls)
1877-1941

m

Rose Wilder Lane
1857-1949

Despite her lack of high school diploma, she taught school from age 15 to 18, when she married Almanzo.

Laura's "farmer boy" husband wooed her through his beloved Morgan horses, driving her home from teaching and taking her on Sunday drives.

Younger sister Carrie's memories were enthusiastically on tap for Laura's books. She was a typesetter and reporter. Her stepson Harold helped carve Mount Rushmore.

"Baby" Grace grew up in the *Little Town on the Prairie*. Like Laura, she taught in the local schools until she married, and wrote for the newspapers.

A reporter and prolific novelist, Rose's post-First World War reporting took her throughout Europe. Later, she helped publish Laura's books and used some of Laura's stories in her own novels.

Mary Amelia Ingalls
1865-1928

Laura's older sister was blind from age 14. Laura's teaching helped support Mary's attendance at the college for the blind in Vinton, Iowa, US.

Mahatma Gandhi~

Until 1948, Mahatma Gandhi was India's spiritual and political leader. His practice of ahimsa (nonviolence) and satyagraha (civil disobedience) influenced policies and inspired activists worldwide. A leader in the Indian National Congress, he worked to end British rule in India, abolish caste discrimination, expand women's rights, and decrease poverty. To achieve this, he organized nonviolent campaigns, where people would do such things as refuse to work, sit in the streets, and boycott the courts.

His most famous campaign was the 240-mile Dandi Salt March of 1930, where he protested the British salt tax. Sadly, India's independence from Britain in 1947 actually led to Pakistan and India becoming divided states, and to religious violence instead of the peace Gandhi had hoped for. In 1948, on his way to a prayer meeting, Gandhi was assassinated by a fellow Hindu.

The Gandhi Family

Around 1700, Gandhi's oldest-known ancestor, Lalji, moved 24 miles from Kutiyana, in Junagadh, to the western coastal city of Porbandar, in Gujarat. There, he entered the service of its ruler, the Rana of Porbandar. The following generations served as civil servants to the state until the 19th century, when Gandhi's grandfather achieved the position of Diwan (Prime Minister). Today, Gandhi's descendants live around the world. Many are activists and politicians, but others are journalists, surgeons, and software engineers.

Lalji Gandhi
c. 1674

Uttamchand Gandhi
c. 1794

Lakshmi Gandhi
c. 1760-1820

Harilal Mohandas Gandhi
1888-1948

Gulab Gandhi
unknown-1918

He was the first Gandhi to be Diwan (Prime Minister). When the regent fired him, he retreated to the ancestral home, which his father had bought. Once reinstated, he passed the Diwan position to his son.

Denied his desire to study law in Britain, Harilal rejected the family. He converted to Islam, drank alcohol, and gambled. He died of tuberculosis, two months after his father.

Putlibai Gandhi
1839-1891

Karamchand Uttamchand Gandhi *1822-1885*

Manilal Gandhi
1892-1956

Sushila Mashruwala Gandhi
1907-1988

Chakravarti Rajagopalachari ("Rajaji" or "C.R.")
1878-1972

m

An extremely religious Hindu, she fasted regularly and taught her children religious tolerance. When Gandhi went to England to study, she worried about loss of caste.

The prime minister of the Porbandar State, he was not formally educated. He learned his job through his father. The family was well-to-do, but not wealthy.

He led Gandhi's fight in South Africa, becoming Editor of the *Indian Opinion*. He was jailed over 25 times while protesting racial discrimination.

Gandhi's colleague in the independence movement, he held numerous political offices. Both fathers imposed a five-year waiting period before their children, Devdas and Lakshmi, could marry.

Mahatma Mohandas Karamchand Gandhi
1869-1948

Kasturbai "Kasturba" Mohandas Gandhi (Kasturbai Makhanji Kapadia) *1869-1944*

Ramdas Gandhi
1898-1969

Nirmala Gandhi
1909-2000

Devdas Mohandas Gandhi
1900-1957

Lakshmi
1912-unknown

m

m

Despite her poor health and chronic bronchitis, she embraced Gandhi's political work, even joining him in jail.

Although he and his wife were born into the wealthy merchant caste, they lived simply, opposing caste discrimination. A London-educated lawyer, he asked his sons to live self-disciplined lives.

Active in his father's movement, his health was destroyed by the protests and jailings of the 1930s. He never embraced Gandhi's ideal of poverty and his wife remained an anti-poverty activist to the end.

He was jailed several times for protest activities. Unlike his brothers, he stayed close to his father, at times as his secretary.

John F. Kennedy

Pulitzer Prize Winner

An erratic student, John did well in English and history but was distracted from duller subjects by the pleasures of a privileged youth. However, his Harvard college thesis, *While England Slept* became a bestseller. Later, he and his aide, Theodore Sorenson, wrote *Profiles in Courage*, which won the Pulitzer Prize for Biography.

"Ask not what your country can do for you: ask what you can do for your country." said John F. Kennedy (JFK), the charismatic young 35th president of the United States, at the close of his 1961 inauguration. JFK was president during the tensions of the Cuban missile crisis, the Space Race, and the construction of the Berlin Wall. At home, his short term in office led to the passing of the Civil Rights Amendment of 1964 and the foundation of the Peace Corps. With his youth and charm and that of his sophisticated wife, Jackie, the White House was at its most glamorous, and he was one of the best loved of the US presidents. His 1963 assassination by communist Lee Harvey Oswald remains a controversial event and was the end of an almost-mythical era.

The Kennedy Family

In the 1840s, a fungus decimated Ireland's vital potato crop. During the ensuing Great Hunger, a million Irish emigrated to the Americas. JFK's Irish great-grandparents all came to Boston. Within two generations, the Kennedy and Fitzgerald families had risen from the East Boston slums, conquering local prejudice against the Irish to become Boston's wealthiest and most influential political families. JFK and his siblings enjoyed privileged childhoods, attended Harvard, and mingled with the social and Hollywood elite.

Bridget Murphy 1821-1888
Patrick Kennedy 1823-1858

James Hickey 1836-1900
Margaret Field 1835-1911

Thomas Fitzgerald 1823-1885
Rosanna Cox 1835-1879

Mary Ann Fitzgerald 1834-1904
Michael Hannon 1832-1900

Patricia Kennedy 1957

Mary Augusta Hickey 1857-1923

John Francis Fitzgerald 1863-1950
Mary Josephine Hannon 1865-1964

Robert Francis Kennedy 1925-1968
Ethel Skakel 1928

Edwin Arthur Schlossberg 1945

Bridget's hard work, savings, and success as a shopkeeper started her son, P.J., on his road to success. Her husband emigrated to East Boston in 1849.

Her parents emigrated from County Cork, Ireland. She married saloon keeper and businessman P.J. Kennedy, raising their large family while he created a comfortable lifestyle.

Known as "Honey Fitz" for his sweetness, John served as a state senator and US congressman, plus two terms as Boston's mayor. He married his second cousin, Mary.

As JFK's brother's Attorney General, "Bobby" managed his campaigns. He was a US senator, activist, and presidential candidate when he was assassinated.

"P.J." Patrick Joseph Kennedy 1858-1987 — m

Joseph Patrick Kennedy 1888-1969

Rose Elizabeth Kennedy (Fitzgerald) 1890-1995

Edward Moore Kennedy 1932-2009

Jean Ann Kennedy 1928
Stephen Edward Smith 1927

Eunice Mary Kennedy 1921-1953
Robert Sargent Shriver 1915-2011

m

P.J. was the first Kennedy with a formal education. Likeable and clever, he became a successful saloon keeper, importer, investor, and politician, serving terms as a US Senator.

A multi-millionaire, he made fortunes in Wall Street and Hollywood. He served as SEC Commissioner and US Ambassador to Great Britain. However, his political ambitions were for his sons.

Deeply religious and calling herself an "old fashioned girl," she was the stoic and resilient matriarch of the family.

"Ted" Kennedy was Democratic Senator for Massachusetts for over 40 years. A spokesman for social welfare legislations and world affairs, he advocated for liberal causes, including housing and voting rights and national healthcare.

John Fitzgerald Kennedy. Jr. 1960-1999
Carolyn Jeanne Kennedy 1966-1999

Joseph Patrick Kennedy. Jr. 1915-1944

John Fitzgerald Kennedy 1917-1963

Jacqueline Lee Bouvier 1929-1994

Kathleen Agnes Kennedy Marchioness of Hartington 1920-1948
William John Robert Cavendish 1917-1944

Rosemary Kennedy 1918-2005

m

His father pinned his presidential hopes on his first-born son, but Joseph "Joe Jr." was shot down in a Second World War bomber over the English Channel.

After Joe Jr's death, "Jack" was the family's next candidate for the presidency. A likeable war hero, he became a US congressman and junior senator en route to the White House.

A well-educated socialite and journalist, "Jackie" brought elegance and fashion to the White House. As First Lady, her interests were the arts and historic preservation.

Three-year-old John's salute at his father's funeral became an icon of stoic loss. A lawyer, he died, along with his wife, Carolyn, and sister-in-law Lauren, when his self-piloted plane crashed off the New England coast.

Nelson Mandela

In 1994, four years after his release from Robben Island prison, Nelson Rolihlahla Mandela was elected president of South Africa. He had been a political prisoner for 27 years, but he pledged to build "a rainbow nation at peace with itself and the world." Fifty years before, Mandela had joined the African National Congress (ANC), taking his law degree into politics. In 1948, the government of South Africa introduced apartheid—a system of racial segregation—and Mandela was arrested as a revolutionary. In prison, Mandela became a powerful anti-apartheid leader with growing international influence. He was released in 1990 and began negotiations to end apartheid. His success earned him the 1993 Nobel Peace Prize, and he remains a beloved and potent symbol of triumph over adversity today.

Ubuntu

Mandela's leadership embraced African Ubuntu philosophy, meaning "human brotherhood." He declared, "Umuntu ngumuntu ngabantu," which means "a person is a person because of other people."

The Mandela Family

Mandela's great-grandfather was the last independent king of South Africa's Thembuland. In the 11th century, ancestor Zwimbe led the cattle-herding Xhosa tribes south from Central Africa, down the eastern coast. By the 1500s, the Thembu had split from KwaZulu-Natal tribes, settling in the Transkei area of East Cape and absorbing local groups, like the Mpondo. In the late 1700s, the Dutch entered Xhosa territory. British settlers followed in 1820.

Jongintaba David Dalindyebo Mtirara
1870-1942

When Mandela's father died, the Regent honored the strong rural tradition of the extended family, accepting Mandela as a son and grooming him for tribal leadership.

Mase (unknown)

Evelyn Ntoko Mase
1922-2004

Zwimbe
11th century

King of Thembu
c. 1832

Nkosi Mphakanyiswa Gadla Hendry Mphakanyiswa
1880-c. 1930

m

Nosekeni Nonqaphi Janny
c. 1851-1968

A devout Methodist, she sent Mandela to the local mission school, where he received his Western name.

Alice Mase Sisulu
c. 1869

Walter Max Ulyate Sisulu
1912-2003

He was a political activist and a mentor to Mandela. A member of the ANC, he helped lead the battle against apartheid.

Thembi died in a car crash, while Makgatho's death was due to AIDs. Maki was named in honor of her sister, who died at 9 months old.

Evelyn met Mandela through her cousin, Mandela's mentor Walter Sisulu. Despite their similar backgrounds, she was not interested in politics.

m

Madiba Thembekile 1945-1969; Makgatho Lewanika Mandela 1950-2005; Makaziwe 1948-1948; Makaziwe (Maki) 1954

A descendant of the "left hand" branch of the Thembu royal family, he was Chief of Mvezo and similar to a Prime Minister.

President Rolihlahla Nelson Mandela
1918-2013

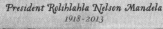

Rolihlahla means "to pull a branch of a tree" or "troublemaker." His four "mothers" were a source of strength—his extended family is large but is divided politically.

Mabel Notancu Timakwe (Mandela)
1886-2002

Leabie Philiso Mandela
1930-1997

The sisters happily recall life in their mother's home. Boys herded cattle while women prepared stone-ground maize mixed with sour milk and cooked in three-legged pots.

m

Graça Machel
c. 1945

Columbus Kokani Madikizela
c. 1874

Zenani Mandela-Dlamini
c. 1959

Zindziswa Mandela-Hlongwane
c. 1960

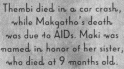

Winifred Nomzamo Zanyiwe Madikizela
1936-2018

m

Gertrude Mzaidume
1874-1944

Both daughters became politicians. Growing up with Mandela in prison and Winnie under house arrest, they were virtual orphans, educated in Swaziland, away from harassment.

They met as activists and spent most of their marriage apart. In prison, Mandela evolved into a statesman, while she became a mentor to the violent younger activists.

The South African government created homelands to segregate black communities. Columbus was a teacher, but later served in the government of the Transkei homeland.

The widow of Mozambique's first president, she married Mandela in 1998. She is a strong humanitarian advocate, especially for children.

Maria Tallchief

When Maria Tallchief was 12 years old, her father told her she must choose between piano or dance. She had studied both passionately since she was three, but she chose dance. When she was eight years old, the family left Oklahoma for the opportunities offered by Hollywood. However, at 17, Maria joined New York City's Ballet Russe de Monte Carlo. Although the company's Russian dancers scorned the Native American, she became the muse of famous choreographer George Balanchine. Later moving to Paris, she faced more prejudice but soon was soloing and winning European hearts with her passionate artistry. Returning to New York, she became Prima Ballerina at the Balanchine Ballet Society—later the New York City Ballet. Her athleticism and style transformed the Euro-centric ballet world, and today she is considered one of the world's greatest dancers.

Famous Roles

Russia dominated the world of ballet. Tallchief's early mentors were Madame Nijinska and David Lichine, both teachers of classical Russian ballet. Russians composed the music that George Balanchine used to create Tallchief's most famous roles—the Firebird, the Swan, and *The Nutcraker's* Sugarplum Fairy. *Nutcracker*, a previously obscure ballet, soon became a Christmas favorite.

Recognition

While a dancer's best award is a lead role, Tallchief has also received an annual Kennedy Center Honor and the National Medal of the Arts. She was one of five Native American ballerinas named Oklahoma Treasures.

The Tallchief Family

Maria's paternal ancestors were members of a Native American tribe known as the Osage Nation. In the 1800s, the US government forced them from their Kansas lands to make room for white settlers. The Osage were moved to Oklahoma's "Indian Territory." However, they were one of the few Native American tribes to still "own" their land. With the help of Maria's great-grandfather, Peter Bigheart, they managed to negotiate with the US government to keep the right to minerals found on their land. So, when oil was discovered in their reservation in 1894, the Osage Nation—Maria's ancestors—became wealthy.

John Anderson Porter I
1826-1900

Thomas A. Hoskinson, Sr.
1679-1743

Thomas Beall
1647-1730

Colonel Ninian Beall
1625-1717

Hun-Ka-Me Bigheart
c. 1826

m

Nun-tsa-turn-kah Bigheart
c. 1819

m

Wah-hiu-shah Bigheart
c. 1827

Thomas A. Hoskinson, Jr.
1719-1802

Chief Woman "Wah-Ko-Ki-He-Kah"
1843-1915

m

Peter Cassidy Bigheart
1839-1915

Chief James Bigheart
1842-1908

Moses Franklin Porter
1693-1776

m

Elizabeth Ann Porter (Hoskins)
1828-1855

John Henry Porter
1849-1910

Mary Ann Beall
1722-1800

m

Colonel Ninian (Ruth's paternal ancestor) was transported to Barbados as a Cromwellian prisoner of war.

m

Marie Antoinette Porter
c. 1863

Tall Chief (first name unknown)
before 1847

Wah-Shah-Hah-Me *c. 1847*

Although baptized a Catholic, Peter was a "blanket" Indian, practising traditional Osage ways. He was a Civil War scout for the Union Army and elected Chief after James Bigheart.

Peter's half brother, a full-blooded Osage, was baptized Catholic and followed Western ways. He was with the Black Beaver Osage Band. Peter was with the William Penn Band.

Ruth Mary Tall Chief (Porter)
1899-1981

Joseph Alexander Tall Chief
1890-1959

Alexander Tall Chief *1866-1910*

Eliza Bigheart *1870-1952*

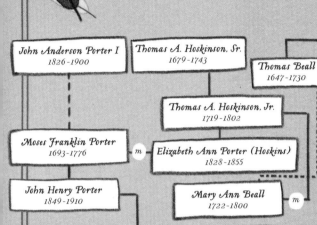

m

George Balanchine
1904-1983

Henry Daniel "Buzz" Paschen
1927-2004

Ruth met Maria's father while visiting her sister, who was the Tall Chiefs' cook and housekeeper. Loving music and dance, she was determined to give her children the chance she never had.

Maria's father grew up rich. As she once said, "As a young girl growing up on the Osage reservation in Fairfax, Oklahoma, I felt my father owned the town."

m

Elmourza Natirboff
1925-2012

He was famous for his musicality and athletic choreography. He also became obsessed with his dancers, including Maria, who was half his age. Their 1946 marriage was annulled in 1952.

He was CEO of Paschen Contractors, Inc., which produced Chicago landmarks like Navy Pier. Maria found his ignorance of ballet "refreshing." They married in 1956. They remained together through his convictions of fraud and tax evasion.

Marjorie Louise Tall Chief
c. 1927

Elizabeth Marie "Betty" Tallchief
1925-2013

m

Elise Paschen
1959

A successful poet and graduate of Harvard and Oxford universities, Dr Paschen teaches at the School of the Art Institute of Chicago. She is an enrolled member of the Osage Nation.

Maria's sister and "best friend," she was the first Native American to become the *premiere danseuse etoile*, or the prima ballerina, in the Paris Opera Ballet. In 1981 she co-founded the Chicago City Ballet with Maria.

Maria combined her last names to avoid teasing in school. She was too proud of her heritage to "Russianize" to Tallchieva but changed her professional name to "Maria." Her Osage name became Wa-Xthe-Thomba, "Woman of Two Worlds."

Martin Luther King, Jr.

Martin Luther King, Jr. dreamed of justice for all. His was the African-American voice of the civil rights movement from 1957-1968. He spoke over 2,500 times at protests like the 1963 March on Washington—the stage for his famous "I Have a Dream" speech. King was born into a family of preachers and activists. He joined his father as co-pastor, but expanded his pulpit to places where African Americans were fighting segregation and discrimination in business, education, and law. Despite threats and violence, he preached nonviolence. This, along with his acceptance of whites, put him at odds with more militant "Black Power" activists.

In 1964, he received the Nobel Peace Prize for his activism, but four years later he was assassinated. A few months later, Congress passed the Civil Rights Act of 1968.

Influences

King's father preached nonviolence. His mother's father preached a social gospel influenced by Booker T. Washington—who supported developing Black businesses—and W.E.B. Du Bois—founder of the NAACP's civil activism. King himself followed Christianity for theory and Gandhi for action.

NAACP, the National Organization for the Advancement of Colored People

A grass-roots civil rights organization, the NAACP was founded in 1909 to provide justice for African Americans. Over 100 years later, it also looks at multi-racial legal, economic, and political issues. King's entire family worked within the NAACP. It has kept its well-known name, despite changes in terminology and focus.

WE DEMAND JOBS FOR ALL NOW!

WE DEMAND JOBS

WE MARCH FO

WE MARCH FO FIRST CLASS CITIZENSHIP NOW!

WE MARCH FOR JOBS

WE DEMAND VOTING RIGHTS

The King Family

Martin Luther King, Jr. mainly descends from African slaves, although his ancestors also include a disinherited English Quaker immigrant, who was likely a servant. King's ancestors were liberated after the Civil War, but, like many former slaves, they kept their owners' surnames and remained on their plantations as sharecroppers. This was a Southern system that provided landless people (usually former slaves) with work and a home, while cash-poor landed people (usually former slave owners) paid the workers in a share of the crops. Black sharecroppers were slaves in everything but name, and subject to violence and racism at the hands of white employers and neighbors.

Nathan King
1830-1880

Malinda King
1846-1880

Jim Long
1842-1880

Jane Linsey
1855-1880

Willis Williams
1810-1874

m

Lucrecia Daniel
1840-unknown

William Parks
1825-unknown

Janzie
1829-unknown

James Albert "Jim" King
1864-1933

m

Delia Linsey King
1875-1924

A slave preacher, he kept his owner's name after he was liberated, working as a sharecropper on the Williams plantation. His son, A.D. followed in his ministerial footsteps.

Rev. Adam Daniel "A.D." Williams
1863-1931

m

Jennie Celeste Parks Williams
1873-1941

A sharecropper of Irish-African descent, his response to poverty and racism was violence, not religion. But he did not prevent his family's church-going.

Of Puritan and African descent, her father, Jim Long, was a former slave. She was a devout Baptist, with an emphasis on nonviolence. She taught her children these values.

He advanced from itinerant minister to an educated and impassioned preacher at Atlanta's Ebenezer Baptist Church. He also founded the local NAACP chapter.

Deeply religious, she was a model "First Lady" of the Church. King's family lived with the Williams grandparents, and he was inconsolable at her death.

Rev. Martin Luther King, Sr.
1899-1984

m

Alberta Christine Williams King
1903-1974

Rev. Martin Luther King, Jr.
1929-1968

Coretta Scott King
1927-2006

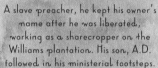

m

While lacking his son's facility with language, "Daddy King" used his pulpit at the huge Ebenezer Baptist Church for 44 years to promote civil rights and nonviolence.

A talented singer, she met King while she was studying music. She played a crucial role in continuing the struggle for racial equality after her husband's death.

"Mama King" was a quietly strong presence. She was shot in place of her husband while playing organ for a Sunday service in 1974.

In 1934, King's father changed both of their names from Michael to Martin Luther. His father also ordained him as a Baptist minister in 1948.

Edythe Scott Bagley
1924-2011

Obadiah Scott *1903-1974*
Bernice MacMurry Scott *1904-1996*

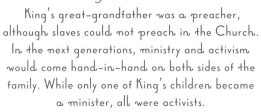

Ministry and Activism

King's great-grandfather was a preacher, although slaves could not preach in the Church. In the next generations, ministry and activism would come hand-in-hand on both sides of the family. While only one of King's children became a minister, all were activists.

A behind-the-scenes activist, writer and educator, she founded the Theater Arts major at Cheyney University and wrote a biography of her sister, Coretta.

Both parents were uneducated but determined their children would go to college. Bernice drove the school bus for all the black segregated teens.

Further Reading

Anderson, William. *Laura's Album: A Remembrance Scrapbook of Laura Ingalls Wilder* New York: Harper Collins, 2016

DK. *100 People Who Made History,* London: DK Children (2012)

DK. *100 Women Who Made History* London: DK Children, 2017

DK. *The Shakespeare Book: Big Ideas Simply Explained* London: DK Children, 2015

Deary, Terry. *Rowdy Revolutions* (Horrible Histories Special) London: Scholastic, 2011

Macy, Sue. *Bull's Eye: A Photobiography of Annie Oakley* Washington: National Geographic Society, 2015

Brimming with creative inspiration, how-to projects, and useful information to enrich your everyday life, Quarto Knows is a favorite destination for those pursuing their interests and passions. Visit our site and dig deeper with our books into your area of interest: Quarto Creates, Quarto Cooks, Quarto Homes, Quarto Lives, Quarto Drives, Quarto Explores, Quarto Gifts, or Quarto Kids.

Inspiring | Educating | Creating | Entertaining

First Published in 2018 by Lincoln Children's Books,
an imprint of The Quarto Group.
The Old Brewery, 6 Blundell Street, London N7 9BH, United Kingdom.
T (0)20 7700 6700 F (0)20 7700 8066 www.QuartoKnows.com

ISBN 978-1-78603-226-3

The illustrations were created watercolor
Set in Woolen and Emblema

Published by Rachel Williams
Designed by Karissa Santos
Edited by Eryl Nash
Production by Jenny Cundill

Manufactured in Guangdong, China

9 8 7 6 5 4 3 2 1

FSC
www.fsc.org
MIX
Paper from
responsible sources
FSC® C104723